The MICHIGAN HISTORICAL REVIEW

Vol. 14   No. 1   Spring   1988

Editor: John D. Haeger, *Central Michigan University*

Book Review Editor: William T. Bulger, *Central Michigan University*

Associate Editors:
Thomas L. Jones, *Historical Society of Michigan*
William H. Mulligan, Jr., *Clarke Historical Library*

Assistant Editor: Sheila McCormick, *Central Michigan University*

Student Assistant: Michele VanBuskirk

The MICHIGAN HISTORICAL REVIEW

The *Michigan Historical Review* (ISSN 0890-1686) was formerly titled, *The Great Lakes Review.* It is now published semiannually by the Clarke Historical Library at Central Michigan University in cooperation with the Historical Society of Michigan. Individual and institutional subscriptions are available for $10 from the Clarke Historical Library, Central Michigan University.

The *MHR* can also be obtained as one benefit of membership in the Historical Society of Michigan. The Historical Society of Michigan is Michigan's state-wide, membership-supported organization devoted to the publication and promotion of Michigan history. Membership in the Society includes as benefits the *Michigan Historical Review* and the bimonthly *Chronicle,* an illustrated Michigan history magazine/ newsletter. Also included is the annual Burton Memorial Lecture. See the inside back cover for additional information about the Historical Society of Michigan.

****

The *Michigan Historical Review* publishes articles relating to Michigan's political, economic, social, and cultural history. The editor also welcomes manuscripts in American, Canadian, and Midwestern history that directly or indirectly explore important themes related to Michigan's past. Articles should be submitted in duplicate and doublespaced, with notes and citations on separate pages. The author's name and address should appear only on a separate title page. Correspondence regarding manuscripts, subscriptions, suggestions for future issues, and all other editorial matters should be addressed to the Editor, *Michigan Historical Review,* Clarke Historical Library, Central Michigan University, Mt. Pleasant, Michigan 48859. (517-774-6567)

****

The *Michigan Historical Review* is not responsible for statements of fact or opinion made by its contributors.

****

Articles appearing in this journal are abstracted and indexed in *Historical Abstracts, America: History and Life,* and *Current Contents.*

****

****

Cover: Flier Advertising Communist Rally Against Michigan's Alien Registration Law of 1931. Courtesy of the Archives of Labor and Urban Affairs, Wayne State University.

The MICHIGAN HISTORICAL REVIEW

Vol. 14   No. 1   Spring   1988

Contents

Labor Market Politics in Detroit:
The Curious Case of the
"Spolansky Act" of 1931

by
Thomas A. Klug

Midway through the 19 June 1931 issue of the *Detroit Labor News*, a bitter exchange appeared between the Detroit Federation of Labor and Rabbi Leon Fram, one of the city's Jewish leaders. Several times in recent weeks the DFL had publicly endorsed an alien registration law that had cleared the Michigan legislature and Governor Wilbur M. Brucker's desk in late May. The measure, which Detroit labor attorney Maurice Sugar at the time penned the "Spolansky Act," originated as a combined anti-alien and anti-communist initiative of the Union League of Michigan, a Detroit-based organization of conservative Republican businessmen and professionals which thrived on ardent opposition to union labor and left-wing radicals. The law required that each of Michigan's 250,000 aliens register with the Commissioner of Public Safety, provide photographic and fingerprint identification, and obtain a certificate that verified their status as a "legal resident of the State." Only under these conditions could aliens reside, sojourn, engage in business or work in Michigan. Employers were required to employ only registered aliens. Further, any alien caught by the police without a valid certificate and unable to establish a right of residence was subject to a fine, ninety days in jail, and then delivery to federal immigration authorities for possible deportation.[1]

Thomas A. Klug is a Ph.D. candidate in history at Wayne State University and currently teaches at Marygrove College. He would like to acknowledge Nora Faires, Christopher Johnson, Rebecca Reed, Rosanne Hostnik and Steve Babson for their help and support. An earlier version of this paper was presented at the Social Science History Association conference in St. Louis, October 1986.

[1] *Detroit Labor News*, 19 June 1931, p. 4; Maurice Sugar, "Michigan Passes the 'Spolansky Act,' " *The Nation* 133 (8 July 1931): 31-33. The Detroit Federation of Labor endorsed the Spolansky Act at meetings on 20 May and 3 June 1931. See *Detroit Labor News*, 22 May 1931, p. 1; and 5 June 1931, pp. 1, 4. Contemporaries generally knew Michigan Public Act No. 241 of 1931 as the

Rabbi Fram recognized that only the apparatus of a police state could carry out the provisions of the law. And he was stunned and bewildered by the DFL's support for this kind of vicious immigrant-bashing. "May I express to you," wrote Fram to the editor of the *Detroit Labor News*, "my profound disappointment at the spectacle of the organized labor of Detroit giving aid and comfort to the czarism, terror, blackmail and extortion which compose the text of Michigan's recently enacted Alien Registration Bill. It is difficult, for me to understand how a group which has suffered from all those evils can so blandly impose them on others. Only a primitive jungle hatred of the alien could have inspired that bill." Not true, countered the DFL. "We want to say very frankly to the Rabbi that there is no primitive jungle spirit in our attitude on this matter, but rather a desire to protect ourselves from the jungle attitude of labor exploiters, and the class of aliens who lend themselves so readily to the machinations of the employers in their desire to destroy American standards."[2]

The response of the DFL to Rabbi Fram points to the importance of the conflicting labor-market interests of organized workers and employers in explaining the origins and complex politics that surrounded this first attempt by a state to impose registration on all of its non-citizen inhabitants.[3] During the first three decades of the century organized workers in Detroit competed with employers for control of the local labor market—a market which during the same period underwent a profound structural change as the automobile industry developed and as migration and immigration channels provided employers with tens of thousands of new workers. The manufacturers won the fight, and generally they were satisfied with extensive labor mobility and corporate autonomy in managing open-shop employment relations.

But the unions persevered, and in their weakened condition they championed stern governmental, administrative, and legislative measures which they hoped might tip the balance of

---

Cheeney Alien Registration Act, after the representative who introduced it into the state house.

    [2] "The Rabbi Rants," *Detroit Labor News*, 19 June 1931, p. 4.

    [3] ACLU, *Daily News Release*, 10 December 1931, *American Civil Liberties Union Records and Publications* (Glen Rock, N.J.: Microfilming Corporation of America, 1977), Reel 3.

power in the labor market in their favor. Thus they wholeheartedly favored the strict enforcement of immigration and anti-convict labor laws, and they rallied to such new ones as Michigan's alien registration act. On its journey to alien registration the DFL met conservative anti-communists of the Union League of Michigan who, in order to strike at immigrants and subversives, pushed for the regimentation of the labor market at the cost of a split with employing interests (as represented by the Michigan Manufacturers Association). The latter, in turn, found unexpected allies among the Communist party, the American Civil Liberties Union, and liberal and immigrant leaders, all of whom resisted the repressive logic entailed by alien registration. Ultimately, the federal judiciary asserted the predominance of the national labor market and, thereby, upheld the political and economic status quo.[4]

At first it may seem quite odd to suggest an accommodation between conservative elements and unions around the Spolansky Act for the simple reason that in the late 1920s and early 1930s labor barely was organized in Detroit. Of course, economically, Detroit was the world's automotive capital. It stood at the hub of a constellation of automobile, body, parts, and accessory plants which revolved within a radius of 250 miles from the city. But Detroit was not only a major industrial center. It was also one of the preeminent open-shop citadels in the United States, the "Capital of Industrial Freedom," as the head of the Employers' Association of Detroit once put it. The automobile industry was foremost among the country's practitioners of unilateral management control over

---

[4] Among the most interesting studies that consider the connections between political behavior and labor-market interests are Edna Bonacich, "A Theory of Ethnic Antagonism: The Split Labor Market," *American Sociological Review* 37 (October 1972): 547-59; Kitty Calavita, "California's 'Employer Sanctions' Legislation: Now You See It, Now You Don't," *Politics and Society* 12 (1983): 205-30, and *U.S. Immigration Law and the Control of Labor, 1820-1924* (Orlando, Fla.: Academic Press, 1984); Gary Cross, *Immigrant Workers in Industrial France: The Making of a New Laboring Class* (Philadelphia: Temple University Press, 1983); Gwendolyn Mink, *Old Labor and New Immigrants in American Political Development: Union, Party, and State, 1875-1920* (Ithaca: Cornell University Press, 1986); and Stan Vittoz, "World War I and the Political Accommodation of Transitional Market Forces: The Case of Immigration Restriction," *Politics and Society* 8 (1978): 49-78.

employment relations. Scarcely a trade union existed among the 285,000 employees of sixteen major automobile and auto-related corporations operating in the Detroit district in late 1928.[5]

But in the interstices of the local labor market, albeit isolated and contained by aggressively anti-union employers, a large number of mainly craft unions continued to survive. Between 1928 and 1931, Detroit city directories listed ninety union locals which fell into six principal categories: construction and building maintenance; metal trades; printing; transportation; food, clothing, and tobacco; and service (restaurants, hotels, theaters, and barber shops).[6] Most of the unions belonged to the Detroit Federation of Labor. It is difficult to determine the membership of organized labor in Detroit in the 1920s. Accurate figures for the DFL and its allied unions are hard to find. Trade unionists and employers each had good reason to play with the numbers. Certainly the membership was small. Even in the good times of the post-World War I economic boom, Chester Culver, general manager of the EAD, estimated that no more than 8 percent of the city's workers were organized—and probably considerably less.[7] In 1927, Machinists Local No. 28, which claimed jurisdiction over the greatest number of automobile workers, was probably the city's largest union with anywhere from 300 to 700 members.[8]

Whatever the exact level, the machinists' union was of little practical consequence and the prospects of the Detroit labor movement were extraordinarily bleak. Paul U. Kellogg, a visitor to the Motor City in 1926-27, captured labor's plight

---

[5] Robert Dunn, "The Auto Industry and Its Workers: Desperate Need For Unionization," *Labor Age* (April 1929): 3-5, 14; Employer's Association of Detroit (hereafter EAD), *Labor Barometer*, 18 September 1928.

[6] *Detroit City Directory, 1928-29*, 2771-72; *Detroit City Directory, 1930-31*, 2669-70.

[7] Culver's confidential report of 23 November 1920 is on pages 906-909 of "Data for the Detroit Newspaper Publishers' Association Regarding Wages in Detroit Industry," in Printers' Union, Box 14, Metro-Detroit AFL-CIO Collection, Wayne State University Archives of Labor and Urban Affairs, Detroit, Michigan. (Hereafter the Metro Detroit AFL-CIO Collection will be referred to as the AFL-CIO Collection and the Wayne State University Archives will be cited as WSU.)

[8] Paul U. Kellogg, "When Mass Production Stalls," *The Survey* (1 March 1928): 724.

better than anyone. Attending a meeting of the Detroit Federation of Labor, Kellogg found the unionists pleased

> over the outcome of a municipal election, which would strengthen them in the public services. The only fly in the ointment was the lament of the custom tailors' delegate that not one of the candidates they had supported wore a suit with a union label on it! The picture I came away with was that of a small group of unionists, who had contrived to build dikes against the undermining tides of non-union workers, employed and unemployed, which surrounded them. Indeed, I could not help but feel that they regarded the semi-skilled workers of the machine shops more as a threat to their security than as a field for missionary effort.[9]

Craft unionism had not always had it so tough in Detroit. From 1896 to 1902, organized workers expressed confidence as they swelled in number and compelled employers to bargain with union business agents. By 1902, upwards of 20 percent of the city's wage earners were unionized. Unionism in the metal trades was especially strong. More than one-third of the workers in the metal trades belonged to unions. Twelve metal trades unions alone—notably among iron molders, metal polishers, pattternmakers, and machinists—accounted for 37 percent of all Detroit's organized workers.[10] Beginning in 1903, however, labor's gains sparked a stirring open-shop counterattack by employers. All unions felt the pressure, but whereas workers and employers in the construction and printing lines maneuvered themselves into a stalemate, metal trades unionists lost the war in 1907 after suffering defeats in a series of decisive strikes.[11] This was significant, for upon the wreckage of metal trades unionism rose such automobile giants as Ford, Packard, Cadillac, Maxwell, Chalmers, and others. In the 1900s and 1910s, these same firms staked out an enormous

---

[9] Ibid., 723-24.

[10] *19th Annual Report of the Bureau of Labor and Industrial Statistics of Michigan* (Lansing: Robert Smith Printing Co., 1902), 35-55; John J. Whirl, Annual Meeting of the EAD, 9 February 1904. The EAD Historical Materials are located at the American Society of Employers in Detroit, Michigan. Hereafter the collection will be cited as EAD Historical Materials.

[11] Allan Nevins and Frank Hill, *Ford: The Times, the Man, the Company* (New York: Scribner's, 1954), 513; Steve Babson, *Working Detroit* (Detroit: Wayne State University Press, 1986), 21.

sphere in the Detroit economy which fixed the ground rules for much of the local labor market.

Many authors have told the story of the rise of the automobile industry and the wholesale transformation of technology, work, and the skill composition of jobs.[12] The automobile industry also transformed the labor market as manufacturers competed for labor among themselves, with body and parts suppliers, and with other economic sectors. Before World War I, automobile firms experienced many uncertainties in a new and rapidly expanding business. Obtaining sufficient numbers of both skilled and unskilled workers was one nagging problem, particularly every spring when automobile production cycles reached high gear and when competition for labor intensified as outdoor construction projects resumed following the winter layoff.[13] Automobile companies fared the best in this rivalry. Many could afford to pay a top wage in order to get the pick of the workers. Consequently wage rates escalated and long remained high in Detroit. Attractive wages and expanding employment opportunities in turn made the city an economic magnet for workers throughout the region—indeed, throughout the trans-Atlantic economy.

The dependence of Detroit businessmen on the labor of immigrants, already well-established in the nineteenth century, deepened after the turn of the century with the rise of the automobile industry. Between 1900 and 1930, when the city expanded from 285,000 to 1,500,000 people, the foreign born constituted between one-quarter and one-third of the population. Immigrants were most heavily concentrated in manufacturing occupations. In 1920, the foreign born made up 44 percent of those employed in the manufacturing sector, and 40 percent in 1930. The automobile industry hired many of

---

[12] Beside Nevins and Hill's first volume on Ford, other studies on the rise of the automobile industry include George S. May, *A Most Unique Machine: the Michigan Origins of the American Automobile Industry* (Grand Rapids: Eerdmans, 1975); Stephen Meyer III, *The Five Dollar Day: Labor Managment and Social Control in the Ford Motor Company, 1908-1921* (Albany: State University of New York Press, 1981); and James M. Laux et al., *The Automobile Revolution: the Impact of an Industry* (Chapel Hill: University of North Carolina Press, 1928), 3-76.

[13] Nevins and Hill, *Ford*, 517-18. See also the newspaper clippings in "Labor–Detroit," Box 5, Accession 940, Ford Archives, Henry Ford Museum, Dearborn, Michigan.

them. In 1917, when the payroll of Ford Motor Company averaged some 36,000, about 60 percent of the employees were foreign born, three-quarters of whom originated in eastern and southern Europe. Of the 64,000 Detroiters employed as laborers or semi-skilled operatives in automobile factories in 1920, 51 percent were foreign born; they comprised 42 percent of 100,000 similiar workers in 1930. Statistics on other occupations also indicate the strong immigrant composition of Detroit's working class. In 1930, the foreign born were 60 percent of the bakers, 59 percent of the masons, 52 percent of the molders, 50 percent of the carpenters, 49 percent of the plasterers, 44 percent of the metal polishers and buffers, and 43 percent of the machinists.[14]

A pre-World War national policy of laissez-faire with respect to European immigration, reinforced by the open shop on the local level, allowed automobile manufacturers unfettered access to migrant and immigrant labor. This enabled employers to establish a new and super-rationalized, capital intensive and union-free industry in Detroit. But not all of Detroit's economic landscape was as thoroughly revolutionized as the automotive sector. Uneven technological development preserved certain points of worker and trade union resistance to employers. Even within the automobile industry the trimmers and painters who worked on bodies retained a capacity and willingness to fight. These highly skilled workers sustained the wartime organizing drive of the Automobile Workers' Union which reached 18,000 members in Detroit before its collapse during the depression in 1920-21.[15]

Well into the 1920s formal resistance to employers remained in sectors where local labor and product markets existed and

---

[14] Jack Russell, "The Coming of the Line: Rationalization and Labor at the Ford Highland Park Plant, 1910-1920," unpublished typewritten manuscript in possession of the author, 61; Nevins and Hill, *Ford*, 648; Department of Commerce, *Fourteenth Census of the United States, 1920: Occupations*, 4:1101-04; *Fifteenth Census of the United States, 1930: Population*, 4:803-05. On the other hand, only 28 percent of the foremen and 25 percent of the manufacturers were foreign born.

[15] On the AWU, see Jack W. Skeels, "Early Carriage and Auto Unions: The Impact of Industrialization and Rival Unionism," *Industrial and Labor Relations Review* 17 (July 1964): 566-83 and Roger Keeran, *The Communist Party and the Auto Workers' Unions* (1980; reprint, New York: International Publishers, 1986), 28-59.

where, as in printing and pattern-making, employers continued
to rely on skilled labor. Services such as restaurants, theaters,
and hotels were vulnerable to union-inspired consumer
boycotts. The building trades, however, were the main site of
prolonged warfare between unions and employers throughout
the decade. Building contractors attempted to roll back
unionism in the early 1920s through local application of the
nationwide American Plan crusade. A Citizens' Committee
partly financed through the EAD warned that "the building
trades are the breeding grounds of unionism. Once this field is
mastered it is a short and quick step to other industries and
complete union domination, with all of its attendant evils."
Nevertheless unions stubbornly persisted. Almost all electrical,
plumbing, and plastering contractors in the mid-1920s operated
on a closed-shop basis, and unions continued to agitate among
bricklayers, carpenters, painters, and sheet metal workers.[16]

In the 1920s, therefore, AFL craft unions carved out niches
beyond the automobile industry. Aware of the determination
and strength of the anti-union opposition, Detroit's few
remaining unionists understood their difficult situation and
quite naturally manifested a raw survival instinct, expressed in
the form of a jealous protection of their "turf." The imbalance
of power between employers and unions guaranteed that
certain forms of conflict tended to appear more often than
others. Jurisdictional rivalries between unions, for example,
were always more common than serious organizing efforts by
the AFL among the proletarians in heavy industry. This was
because craft labor's fundamental orientation of the decade was
defensive, attuned to assuring the collective survival of the
unionized minority rather than promoting working-class
organization and solidarity. The AFL's strategy amounted to
protecting a privileged stratum of unionized tradesman,
besieged in their local labor markets, from various challenges
to their institutions.[17] Here the swirling mass of unskilled and

---

[16] Babson, *Working Detroit*, 48-50; Robert W. Dunn, *The Americanization
of Labor: The Employers' Offensive Against the Trade Unions* (New York: In-
ternational Publishers, 1927), 21-36, 64-66; Minutes of the EAD Executive
Board, 8 February 1924, EAD Historical Materials.

[17] Babson, *Working Detroit*, 50; James O. Morris, *Conflict Within the AFL:
A Study of Craft Versus Industrial Unionism, 1901-1938* (1958; reprint,
Westport, Conn.: Greenwood, 1974), 55-85. In *Old Labor and New Immig-*

semiskilled industrial workers appeared as a menace to union workingmen. Here, too, immigrants entered as a special problem.

One cannot fully understand the role of immigrants in the AFL's labor-market defense strategy of the 1920s unless one realizes that the immigration restriction acts of 1921 and 1924 significantly altered the struggle between organized labor and employers for control of the American labor market. Part of the debate concerning United States immigration policy since the 1880s had been between employing interests which favored unrestricted immigration and the AFL which eventually came to demand a total ban. Conservative ideological and political forces, strengthened immeasurably by wartime and post-war fears of enemy aliens and left-wing radicals, settled the debate with the passage of immigration restriction or quota legislation.[18] Once done, the center of contention between labor and capital shifted to the administration of the immigration laws: between employers' demands for a "flexible" policy which would open and close the country's borders according to the fluctuating demand for labor, and organized labor's insistence on the rigorous enforcement of the immigration laws and the plugging of loopholes.[19] And, in fact, there were major openings that worried unionists. The most significant gap was the exemption of the native born of Western Hemisphere countries from quota regulations. This not only gave native-born Mexicans and Canadians legitimate access to the United States, but it made the long borders with Mexico and Canada obvious points of entry for European nationalities restricted by law. In Detroit, the control of immigration from Windsor became a test of strength between entrenched unionists and the mighty open-shop employers.

---

rants, Gwendolyn Mink examines for the late-19th century the labor-market roots of the AFL's defensive strategy and its bearings on AFL political behavior.

[18] The following examine the political backround to 1920s immigration restriction: Calavita, *U.S. Immigration Law and the Control of Labor,* 138-61; Robert H. Zieger, *Republicans and Labor, 1919-1929* (Lexington: University of Kentucky Press, 1969), 79-86; and Vittoz, "World War I and Political Accommodation of Transitional Market Forces," 63-78.

[19] EAD, *Industrial Barometer,* February 1923, 3; August 1923, 2; January 1924, 3; EAD, *Annual Report of the General Manager for the Year 1923,* 10-11.

Employers felt that they too had cause to worry about the administration of the immigration laws. After all, the Immigration Bureau was part of the Department of Labor which business representatives, even during the Republican presidencies of the 1920s, considered little more than an AFL encampment within the federal bureaucracy. When the 1921 and 1924 acts further "nationalized" immigration and confirmed its regulation by the Department of Labor, employers in Detroit discovered that law-minded local unionists could put pressure on the immigration bureaucracy to make the system occasionally work on labor's behalf. A strike by metal polishers in 1925 at the C.B. Shepard Company and another of carpenters against the Vokes & Schaffer Company in 1926 gave occasion for the Detroit Federation of Labor to use its influence among immigration officials to have Canadian "scabs" deported on grounds ranging from violations of the contract labor law to the likelihood that the strike-breakers would become "public charges" if injured in strike-related violence.[20]

Despite their complaints about the country's new immigration policies, Detroit employers had little difficulty obtaining workers throughout the 1920s. One reason was that immigration still occurred, especially along the American-Canadian frontier. Legal immigration into the United States averaged 300,000 per year from 1925 to 1929, and 28 percent of it originated in Canada. The same newspapers that told of illicit liquor shipments from Canada into the United States also frequently reported alien smuggling rings located on both sides of the border, often entailing the corruption of Immigration Bureau agents.[21]

The DFL became obsessed with the thought of a breach in the wall against foreign labor caused by lax enforcement on the part of immigration authorities. Labor usually tied violations of the immigration laws to an alleged employers' scheme to flood the local market in order to drive down wages, degrade

---

[20] Chester Culver to Senator James Couzens, 1 September 1926, EAD Historical Materials.

[21] Department of Commerce, *Historical Statistics of the United States, 1789-1945* (Washington, D.C.: Government Printing Office, 1949), 35; "Smuggling Aliens Over the Line: Some Tricks of the Trade," *Literary Digest* 95 (1 October 1927); 50-54

working conditions, and intensify job competition among workers. Frank Martel, a member of Typographical Union No. 18 and president of the DFL, argued that the city was a trade union desert precisely because "of these violations of the immigration law [which] contribute largely to the over-supply of cheap labor" in the district.[22] Gradually, however, Martel and the DFL went beyond looking at breakdowns in the administration of the law and arrived at a second explanation for the plight of Detroit's unionists: the immigration laws as constituted were intrinsically flawed and consequently failed to protect American workers. Thus began Martel's quest for new and tough legal measures to fill the regulatory void.

Between 1926 and 1929, the DFL expended great energy trying to patch up holes in the immigration dike that permitted naturalized Canadians and aliens residing in Windsor to commute daily across the narrow Detroit River to jobs in the United States. The DFL charged that many of the 15,000 to 20,000 commuters were really Europeans and therefore were excludable under the immigration quotas of their respective countries of origin. Yet, every day the DFL saw them illegally cross into the United States where they took the jobs of Americans at lower wages, sometimes finding employment as strikebreakers. In late 1926 and early 1927, the DFL and AFL together lobbied the Department of Labor to remove the "temporary visitor" status of non-native-born Canadian commuters. Their persistence proved successful when the Bureau of Immigration issued General Order No. 86, effective 1 April 1927, which reclassified these particular commuters as "aliens of the immigrant class" and required them to obtain visas and pay head taxes in order to continue working in the United States.[23]

This did not end the matter, and by the fall of 1929 the DFL's stance on immigration and aliens had become more virulent than before. According to Martel, both the 1924 immigration act and General Order No. 86 failed to protect Detroit's workers from foreign labor competition. At the 1929

---

[22] American Federation of Labor, *Report of the Proceedings of the Annual Convention, 1927* (Washington, D.C.: Law Reporter Printing Co., 1927), p. 261. [Hereafter cited, AFL Convention, *Proceedings,* with specific year.]

[23] Correspondence and newspaper clippings appear in Immigration, Box 5, AFL-CIO Collection.

Convention of the AFL in Toronto, Martel cosponsored a resolution urging the revocation of Order 86, claiming that it hardly put a dent in the daily traffic of aliens from Windsor. In fact, argued Martel, the general order had simply legitimized commuting. Later at the same convention Martel went one step further when he alone expressed anger that the gathered delegates had not demanded that the United States Congress apply quota legislation to native-born Canadians—a sensitive topic because of the more than one-quarter million Canadians who were members of international unions affiliated with the AFL.[24]

It was Martel's call at the AFL's 1929 convention for the compulsory registration of all aliens that showed how far he was prepared to go with a strategy of craft labor-market defense. From 1923 to 1927, successive AFL conventions had reacted to alien registration bills before Congress by taking unambiguous and principled positions against them, calling registration "czarist terrorism," a violation of American traditions of liberty, an overture to a system of anti-labor espionage, and a danger to all workers, including the native born. In 1929 the AFL Executive Council began to modify its line when it proposed the compulsory registration of incoming immigrants, but left it voluntary for aliens already living in the country. This was as far as the AFL would go. President William Green drew the line at "extreme measures" involving universal registration of aliens, fingerprinting, and photographing. But at the Toronto convention Martel insisted that universal and compulsory registration was an ideal and useful method of discovering illegal immigrants. Registration, he trusted, would shift the burden of proof of legal entry onto the alien. Lack of papers on the part of an alien would constitute prima facie evidence of illegal entry and warrant immediate deportation. Besides, the registration of aliens was only fair since native-born Americans had their births, marriages, and deaths documented. Only guilty aliens had something to fear. "What is there," asked Martel, "about the

---

[24] 1928 AFL Convention, *Proceedings*, 298-99, 307-9. Martel's resolution failed to pass the Committee on Resolutions. In 1927, the Committee on Resolutions rejected the application of quotas to native-born Canadians. See the 1927 AFL Convention, *Proceedings*, 338.

registration of aliens who are in this country that we are afraid of?"[25]

The logic of the DFL's support for the Spolansky Act of 1931 was thus in place just before the start of the Great Depression. A special combination of the power of Detroit's employers, the craft unionist strategy of defending local labor-market bastions, and the city's attractiveness to immigrants and commuters from Canada brought the DFL to the extreme demand for alien registration.

But the DFL never prepared a registration bill—employers did. Or, to be exact, employers defined an alien problem and began the political process that resulted in the 1931 Michigan act. The trouble that employers had with aliens was not that they competed with American workers for jobs, which was fine enough, but that too many communists were foreign born. This was one of the conclusions of an investigation undertaken in early 1927 by Jacob Spolansky for a committee of Detroit manufacturers connected to the EAD.[26] Spolansky, a pre-war immigrant from the Ukraine, came to Detroit as a special representative of the National Metal Trades Association, an open-shop organization based in Chicago with branches in over a score of northern industrial cities east of the Mississippi River. (The Detroit branch operated through the offices of the EAD; Chester Culver, general manager of the EAD, was the NMTA branch secretary). The NMTA provided its branches and company members with expert services, ranging from machine-shop tips and legal advice to plant guards, undercover spies, and strikebreakers.[27]

In Jacob Spolansky the NMTA and the manufacturers of Detroit found the embodiment of America's first generation of professional radical hunters. A true specialist in the art and methods of domestic counterintelligence, Spolansky was proof

---

[25] 1929 AFL Convention, *Proceedings*, 81-82, 229-32.

[26] W.A. Wheeler, chairman of the special committee of Detroit manufacturers investigating radical organizations and activities, presented the results of the Spolansky investigation to the EAD Executive Board on 24 March 1927. The Spolansky report is located in the minutes of that meeting. (Hereafter it will be cited as the "Spolansky Report.")

[27] On the activities of the NMTA, see U.S. Congress, Senate, Committee on Education and Labor, *Violations of Free Speech and Rights of Labor, Hearings Before a Subcommittee of the Committee on Education and Labor*, part 3, 75th Cong., 1st sess., 1937.

Courtesy of *The Detroit News*

Jacob Spolansky, ca. 1938

that career anti-communists were not born to that role—they
were made. During World War I, the Army's Military
Intelligence Division recruited Spolansky to help uncover
disloyal activities in Chicago (where he was the publisher of a
pro-war and pro-Kerensky Russian-language newspaper).
During his brief service with the MID's Negative Branch,
Spolansky gained valuable firsthand experience controlling a
network of agents and informants, penetrating immigrant
neighborhoods and political organizations, and working with
various civilian and military offices involved in monitoring and
suppressing dissent. Quite naturally after the war he became a
special agent of the Bureau of Investigation of the United
States Justice Department. In his capacity from 1919 to 1924
as head of the Chicago district of the bureau's General
Intelligence Division, Spolansky for the first time labored
directly against the radical left, gathering evidence to jail or
deport "anarchists, communists, and other subversive
elements." With J. Edgar Hoover's GID, Spolansky also learned
that communism was really an international conspiracy
orchestrated by Moscow. In 1920 he took charge of the Palmer
Raid arrests in Chicago, and in 1922 led a raid against the
secret Communist party convention in Bridgman, Michigan.[28]

In 1924 the new attorney general, Harlan Fisk Stone, drew a
halt to the self-declared and illegal anti-radical operations of
the General Intelligence Division. Essentially, an
uncontrollable GID had become an issue of public debate and
hence a political liability. Stone ordered the dismantling of the
GID and instructed the Bureau of Investigation to restrict itself
to criminal (not political) investigations and to violations of
federal law (for which belonging to the Communist party was
not one since there were no federal sedition or criminal
syndicalism statutes). America's capacity to target left-wing
radicals appeared to wither away as Spolansky, like other
federal agents groomed for a career in domestic
countersubversion, suddenly found themselves without jobs.
But the personnel of the secret political police establishment
regrouped. After 1924 they simply transferred their talents and
enthusiasm for chasing subversives to private industry, trade
associations (like the NMTA), and state and municipal police

---

[28] Jacob Spolansky, *The Communist Trail in America* (New York: MacMillan, 1951), 1-30.

"red squads." In the private sector they continued basically
intact as a network which maintained informal liasons with
federal civil and military bureaucracies. As a nationwide
fraternity they unceasingly warned the citizenry about the
"Red Menace" (as Spolansky did with a series of twenty-four
articles in the *Chicago Daily News*) and used the threat of
radical subversion to pressure Congress to provide money and a
legal mandate for a renewed federal role in fighting
communism.[29]

Spolansky arrived in Detroit in January 1927, following a
stint in Passaic, New Jersey, where he aided textile
manufacturers battling the first communist-led mass strike in
the United States.[30] What disturbances in the open-shop
tranquility of Detroit necessitated Spolansky's services? For
one thing, the American Federation of Labor resolved at its
October 1926 convention in Detroit to undertake the
organization of the automobile industry.[31] Although no serious
unionization drive materialized, manufacturers found that the
AFL declaration coincided with increased activity on the part
of communists in Detroit.

Communists moved along a broad front in 1926. That year
communists took over the shattered remnants of the
Automobile Workers' Union, the only industrial union among
auto workers. They also stepped up their pressure within
unions affiliated with the AFL, leading manufacturers to
conclude that communists controlled the local machinists'
union. More troubling was the underground publication and
dissemination of communist shop papers which challenged the
ideological hegemony that employers tried to exercise over
their work forces. The first of more than a dozen papers, the
Ford Worker appeared in April 1926, and within a year it
probably had 6,000 readers.[32]

---

[29] Frank J. Donner, *The Age of Surveillance: The Aims and Methods of
America's Political Intelligence System* (New York: Vintage, 1981), 46-48;
Spolansky, *The Communist Trail*, 10-11.

[30] Spolansky, *The Communist Trail*, 44-45. Albert Weisbord, the leader of
the Passaic strike, followed Spolansky to Detroit in the fall of 1927 when he
became the Communist party's new district organizer.

[31] On the AFL automobile campaign, see Morris, *Conflict Within the AFL*,
57-63; Keeran, *The Communist Party*, 49-51; and John W. Lowe, "Detroit a
Sterile Field for Organized Labor," *The Annalist* (12 November 1926): 629-31.

[32] On communists in Detroit in the 1920s, see Keeran, *The Communist*

All these activities, according to Spolansky, were indicative of a major reorganization underway within the American Communist party, its so-called "Bolshevization" or transformation from a loose and undisciplined federation of foreign-language organizations (a structure derived from the Socialist party) to a more centralized apparatus rooted in factory and neighborhood units, or nuclei. "This arrangement," Spolansky observed, "seems to be technically superior, more flexible and more responsive and alive to the problems of the foreign-born workers than was the old." Bolshevization indeed proved effective for Detroit communists. Their membership figures and the number and circulation of shop papers increased. More importantly communists constructed a rudimentary·base in some of the city's largest factories. By 1929 more than half of the local party's 600 members belonged to a dozen shop nuclei. The party could also count on an unstated number of sympathizers and on more than 10,000 members of ethnic fraternal organizations and workers' clubs which were "dominated by the communists."[33]

In the late-1920s, therefore, the communists had a small but established presence in Detroit industry. Communists not only vigorously propagated the causes of industrial unionism and working-class solidarity, but they also had begun to build an infrastructure that linked the institutions of the party with workplace struggles and the social and mutual benefit organizations of the foreign born. Immigrants made up most of the members and supporters of American communism. This was a fact not lost on Spolansky, who recommended that Detroit's captains of industry wage an aggressive propaganda campaign in foreign-language and factory employees' publications and describe how "the Radical movement is directed against our existing form of government, our industrial system, property rights, homes and religion." He also

---

Party, 28-59; Kellogg, "When Mass Production Stalls," 724-25; and autobiographical accounts by Steve Nelson et al., *Steve Nelson: American Radical* (Pittsburgh: University of Pittsburgh Press, 1981), 29-52; and Vera Buch Weisbord, *A Radical Life* (Bloomington: Indiana University Press, 1977), 146-52.

[33] "Spolansky Report;" Keeran, *The Communist Party,* 38, 43-44; Theodore Draper, *American Communism and Soviet Russia* (1960; reprint, New York: Octagon, 1977), 152-67, 186-209.

called upon manufacturers to sponsor a permanent countersubversion operation with a view "to the securing of such evidence as we can against prominent leaders in the movement" who were vulnerable to deportation.[34]

But no "Red Scare" came of Spolansky's investigation in the late 1920s because manufacturers did not want one. Spolansky's undercover work had obtained the names, addresses, and places of employment of 170 active communists and information regarding some 3,000 others.[35] While firing a handful of agitators presented no problem for employers, spokesmen for industry such as Chester Culver of the EAD found manufacturers in a dilemma when it came to promoting anti-communism. They were caught between the need to preserve the economic status quo, which was so profitable, and the political imperatives of anti-communism. To maintain business confidence Culver had to allay fears that Detroit's open-shop industrial system was susceptible to attack. The EAD had, after all, spent a lot of time and money over the years fostering the belief that Detroit was an invincible open-shop town, that it was a safe place to make long-term investments, and that unions and radicals need not waste their time there. It was doubly important to convey the message to radicals and trade unionists that employers were not worried about keeping things under control. Signals of weakness and vulnerability could result in a terrible miscalculation on the part of Detroit's enemies who might think that the time was ripe for unionization. Hence, Culver tended to minimize the threat of communism and counseled restraint. Culver insisted in 1928 that "no one thoroughly familiar with the [communist] movement and its progress has any fear that it will submerge our system of Government and our industries as it has those of Russia unless we are careless and fail to take ordinary precautions."[36]

, On the other hand, employers understood that the fabulous wealth that accrued from Detroit's reputation for industrial stability really hinged on their control over both the labor market and the large labor force that produced automobiles and erected the city's factories and office buildings.

---

[34] "Spolansky Report."
[35] Ibid.
[36] EAD, *Annual Report of the General Manager for the Year 1927*, p. 12.

Unfortunately, this same labor force primarily consisted of immigrants and their children who were also the support base for communism. So while manufacturers grew rich and powerful through the labor of these workers, the process had its destabilizing side as well.

To insure themselves against subversion, manufacturers appealed to the professional counterintelligence establishment. This gave Spolansky and his compatriots the opening they required. For they deperately needed, and therefore promoted, businessmen's fears of communist infiltration in order to fund, legitimize, and perhaps someday legalize the red-catching network. Alarmed industrialists gave sustenance to this network and, thereby, nurtured a virulently anti-communist ideological and political force which did not respect the special interests of employers. The private agenda of the countersubversive network recognized few limits in the war against world communism. It consistently championed various legal and extra-legal measures directed against the Communist party and its press, against radicals employed in industry, and against aliens. But industrial interests did not relish assuming the costs of a permanent war on communism. They did not welcome a climate of uncertainty and instability that a Red Scare would create, especially if confined to Detroit. And as employers of immigrant labor they did not cherish the thought of surrendering any of their wide-ranging prerogatives on who they could or could not hire.

For a period of time employers managed to restrain die-hard anti-communists—until 6 March 1930, when Communist parties throughout the world organized impressive unemployment demonstrations. In Michigan rallies appeared in Kalamazoo, Grand Rapids, Muskegon, and Hamtramck. Fifteen thousand protestors turned out in Flint. In Detroit, a police force of some 3,600, including mounted and motorcycle units, broke up a crowd of 50,000 to 100,000 people who filled the downtown area at the appointed hour. The immensity and geographic scope of the protests seemed evidence enough of the growing capacity of communists to coordinate their activities and attract thousands of discontented persons.[37]

---

[37] Keeran, *The Communist Party,* 67; Babson, *Working Detroit,* 54-55. Daniel J. Leab explores the 6 March demonstrations and their significance,

The March 6th mobilization galvanized a new special
committee of the United States House of Representatives
created to investigate domestic communism. The underlying
goal of the committee chaired by New York Republican
Hamilton Fish, Jr., was to catalyze political pressure to restore
a counterintelligence mission for the Bureau of Investigation.
Thus the Fish Committee toured the country and amassed
evidence from an array of patriots, businessmen, an occasional
trade union leader, and expert anti-communists. The
investigation activated the anti-radical establishment that had
grown up since the World War. A visit to a city by the
committee was an occasion for public and private surveillance
agencies to display their accumulation of documents and
dossiers on radicals and their organizations.[38]

In late July 1930, the Fish Committee spent two days in
Detroit listening to police chiefs and detectives, corporation
executives, and NMTA emissary Jacob Spolansky. Spolansky
and others established that dues-paying membership in the
Detroit district of the Communist party had grown to between
1,500 and 2,000. Within Detroit proper they belonged to nearly
fifty shop and street units. Added to this were 7,500 to 8,000
"communist members of the language or racial groups."
Witnesses placed special emphasis on the linkage between
foreign-born Slavs, Hungarians, and Russian Jews and the
Communist party. Spolansky estimated that while the
leadership elements of the party were 90 percent native born,
the rank and file was 85 to 90 percent foreign.[39]

Committee members also heard with cynical delight
testimony to the effect that federal as well as local authorities
did not posess adequate legal means to identify, punish, and
deport subversives. The federal government barely helped since
the Department of Justice did not have the authority to

---

however fleeting, for the American Communist party in " 'United We Eat':
The Creation and Organization of the Unemployed Councils in 1930," *Labor
History* 8 (Fall 1967): 300-315.

  [38] Donner, *The Age of Surveillance*, 48-50, 386-87; Spolansky, *The
Communist Trail*, 90.

  [39] Spolansky's testimony is in U.S. Congress, House, Special Committee on
Communist Activities in the United States, *Investigation of Communist
Propaganda, Hearings Before a Special Committee To Investigate Communist
Activities in the United States,* 71st Cong., 2d sess., 1930, Part 4, 1: 174-202.

conduct political operations. Witnesses further alleged that the federal deportation machinery had broken down due to a lack of staff and money. Nor did state criminal syndicalism and red flag laws fill in the gap. Faced with such an overwhelming crisis in combatting communism police authorities felt justified taking the law into their own hands. For example, Flint's police chief, Caesar J. Scavarda, accused Detroit-based communists of instigating a major strike in June among Fisher Body workers. "It is individuals who are making it their business to go from one part of the State to the other, and from one State to another, to create trouble and to disaffect people," said Scavarda. Only police operating outside the law could effectively deal with communists who traveled about the country almost undetected. As Scavarda remarked, "communists come in to violate the law and they cannot be stopped unless I , violate the law myself." The assistant prosecuting attorney for the City of Pontiac testified as to how well illegal tactics worked. He related that Pontiac police arrested on spurious grounds a dozen leading Communists the week before the March 6th demonstrations. "We took them to jail, one in each jail of the different towns—and we have 15 towns here—and we kept them there, separated, and they did not have any demonstration."[40]

The appearance of the Fish Committee in Detroit enhanced the political weight of local countersubversives while it weakened the influence of employers over the political direction of anti-communism. It also inspired the Union League of Michigan to launch its own investigation into communism. This staunchly Republican civic and social men's organization developed in 1928 out of the merger of the Detroit Union League Club (founded in 1922) with the new Michigan-wide body. By 1931 the Union League had more than a thousand members, including the governor of Michigan, Wilbur M. Brucker, and numerous directors and executives of banks, insurance companies, and manufacturing corporations. Chester Culver and George Grant of the EAD were members, as were leaders of the Michigan Manufacturers Association. Arthur Waterfall, a director of the MMA, was a Union League vice president. Hal P. Smith, MMA general counsel, was one of the

---

[40] *Investigation of Communist Propaganda,* 15-16, 132.

league's twenty-seven directors, as were Charles S. Mott and William and Lawrence Fisher, all vice presidents of General Motors.[41]

The conduct of the Union League's investigation fell to its fifteen-member Committee on Subversive Activities, among whom were Chester Culver and vice chairman Jacob Spolansky. The committee conducted public hearings in late 1930 and early 1931 and heard presentations from half a dozen experts. Spolansky made two addresses. In one he warned his audience that communists, if successful, "will destroy the present institutions, eliminate all public officials, liquidate your conception of family life, forbid you to worship the Divine Creator, conscript your competence, and exterminate every semblance of individual initiative." For Spolansky, communism was a profoundly menacing challenge to Judaeo-Christian civilization. Culver likewise appeared and lectured on "The Effect of the Communistic Movement Upon Detroit Industries." He pointed to communist-inspired efforts to ruin factory efficiency and plant morale through acts of sabotage and "sporadic strikes." But Culver also tried to introduce an element of calm when he defended free speech for communists ("as long as a man keeps within the strict limits of the law"), and added his assessment that communist activities of the day "do not, in my opinion, constitute very much of a menace to our civilization or to the present order."[42]

The recommendations of the Committee on Subversive Activities announced at the end of February 1931, amounted to a declaration of war on the Communist party. On combatting domestic communism the Union League's legislative proposals were virtually the same as those that the Fish Committee released in mid-January: the exclusion and deportation of communist aliens; the denaturalization of foreign-born communists; the prohibition of communist publications from

[41] Detroit Union League Club and Union League of Michigan, Miscellaneous Files, Burton Historical Collection, Detroit Public Library; Sugar, "Michigan Passes the 'Spolansky Act,' " 32; *Bulletin of the Union League of Michigan,* 1 (1931): 6.
[42] Jacob Spolansky, "Underground Bolshevism," *Bulletin of the Union League of Michigan,* 1 (1931): 1; Chester M. Culver, "The Effect of the Communistic Movement Upon Detroit Industries," *Bulletin of the Union League of Michigan,* 1 (1931): 4.

the mail and from transportation across state lines; and the outlawing of the Communist party. The Union League went even further and called for the disenfranchisement of native-born citizens who were members of the Communist party and, in the absence of federal leadership in fighting communism, for the registration of aliens in Michigan.[43]

Accordingly, the Union League prepared an alien registration bill—the Spolansky Act—sometime between late-February and 10 April when representative Charles Cheeney of Chesaning introduced it into the state house. W.D. Edenburn, an automobile dealers' lobbyist and a director of the Union League, guided the bill in the legislature where it sailed through without any public hearings or debate. On 11 May it passed the House eighty-two to nine. And with an immediate effect clause the bill cleared the Senate on 18 May on a vote of twenty-three to three, prompting Senator Chester Howell of Saginaw to declare afterwards, "this legislation is badly needed in Michigan. Communists are threatening even now to march to Lansing from Detroit, Pontiac, and Flint to create a demonstration. This bill will give the police authority to deal with the situation in a proper manner." Governor Brucker signed the bill on 29 May and claimed that the law was a necessary piece of protective welfare legislation—for unemployed workers because the removal of illegal aliens would make jobs available for "those who are here lawfully," and for patriotic Americans because the elimination of "undesirable aliens" would bring relief "from the criminal and seditious conduct of those who have no right in this country."[44]

Senator Howell's review of the bill indicated that, while enacted for the vague purpose of "maintaining the economic, industrial, and political welfare of this State,"[45] for its sponsors the welfare of the state meant something quite specific. For the Union League of Michigan, the goal of alien registration was the liquidation of communism in Michigan's industrial cities by

---

[43] "Report of the Committee on Subversive Activities, 27 February 1931, *Bulletin of the Union League of Michigan*, 1 (1931): 5; *New York Times*, 18 January 1931, sec. 1, pp. 1, 24.

[44] *Journal of the House of Representatives*, 11 May 1931, p. 1200-1; *Journal of the Senate*, 18 May 1931, p. 1047; *Detroit News*, 19 May, p. 36, and 30 May 1931, p. 2.

[45] Section I of Michigan Public Act No. 241 of 1931.

striking at the immigrant working-class base of the Communist party. Technically the act involved only the 241,000 aliens in the state (4.98 percent of the population).[46] It attempted to make employment and residence in Michigan virtually impossible for undesirable aliens. Ideally, unwanted aliens would steer clear of Michigan. Those that did enter, however, would be caught, convicted, and then handed over to federal immigration officials for deportation from the country.

The problem was that not all communists were aliens. Nevertheless, the Spolansky Act could have given police the means to reach radicals who were naturalized or native-born citizens. Although registration seemed to concern only aliens, in practice it would have left citizens perhaps more defenseless than aliens from sudden police search and seizure. This was because the act justified police questioning and demanding proof of registration from anybody they suspected was an alien—that is, anybody who appeared, spoke, or behaved like a foreigner, or whom police wanted to harass and detain in jail for some period of time. Obviously naturalized and native-born citizens would have trouble proving their innocence since they would have no reason to possess certificates of legal residence. Eventually they, too, would have to carry some sort of documentation. Thus, the registration of aliens implied—and unleashed—political surveillance over the entire population (4.8 million), which was the standing objective of such militant anti-communists as Jacob Spolansky. This totalitarian quality is what turned mere alien registration, in conjunction with fingerprinting and photographing, into such a formidable instrument of political repression. It made possible the systematic identification of communists, communist sympathizers, union agitators, and strikers. It neutralized the ability of radicals to travel, adopt pseudonyms, and merge imperceptibly into immigrant neighborhoods and the labor

---

[46] *Fifteenth Census of the United States, 1930: Population*, 3: 1115, 1140. Fifty-three percent of Michigan aliens of age 21 years and older lived in Detroit and surrounding Wayne County, where 56 percent of the state's foreign born resided. But by taking aim at aliens the Spolansky Act also primarily targeted women. Statewide, 60 percent of all aliens were female and 40 percent male (a change from a near even balance in 1920). In Wayne County, 45 percent of 187,000 foreign-born women ages 21 and older were aliens, but only 18 percent of 242,000 foreign-born men.

force. And it warranted the formation of a central file system, or political blacklist, under the control of the state police.[47]

Frank Martel and many of the delegates to the Detroit Federation of Labor must have been altogether surprised when they discovered that an alien registration bill passed in—of all places—Lansing. For years they had watched similar legislation wither and die in Congress. The Spolansky Act for the DFL represented the fulfillment of Governor Brucker's campaign promise of 1930 to do something extraordinary for the economically distressed workers of Michigan.[48] The law must also have appeared as a godsend to Detroit unionists who, once again, had become agitated over the issue of Canadian commuters. Beginning in the autumn of 1930, the DFL mounted another campaign to pressure officials in Washington, Lansing, and Detroit to stop the continuing influx of commuters from Windsor, the level of which was down already nearly 80 percent from 1927 because of the depression. Commuters, as cheap alien labor, took the jobs of American workers, the DFL argued, and left American citizens to pay taxes to support the unemployed. Commuters who spent their earnings in Canada also hurt Detroit merchants.[49] Frank Martel, therefore, claimed to act on behalf of the city's general welfare when he sponsored a successful resolution at October's AFL convention which called for the abolition of commuting privileges from Canada. The *Detroit Labor News* hailed it as a grand victory for Detroit, "coming after many years of agitation by Detroit labor representatives."[50]

While the DFL labored for the common good, during these same months preceding the Spolansky Act it blamed Detroit's high rate of unemployment on the "Selfish and reactionary interests," the "silk-stocking aggregation," and the "Open Shop Moguls." The DFL documented the steady efforts made by

---

[47] Sugar, "Michigan Passes the 'Spolansky Act,'" 33; *Detroit News*, 31 May 1931, p. 2.

[48] "Labor Wants Brucker," *Detroit Labor News*, 31 October 1930, p. 1.

[49] "Government Should Act Now" and "American Jobs for U.S. Citizens," *Detroit Labor News*, 24 October 1930, 1. Commuter statistics appear in the issue of 26 December 1930, p. 1.

[50] 1930 AFL Convention, *Proceedings*, 161, 334; "Demand Alien Workers Be Barred," *Detroit Labor News*, 17 October 1930, p. 1.

narrow-minded employers to flood the local labor market.[51] The
Detroit Labor News found more evidence of the betrayal of the
public interest by employers when, in November, it reported
the first major rift between labor and business on the Mayor's
Unemployment Committee, noting the vote in favor of
commuting from Canada by Chester Culver of the EAD and
John Lovett of the MMA, both of whom sat on the 20-odd
person advisory committee opposite Martel and three other
union representatives.[52]

Such was the backdrop when the Spolansky Act became
widely known after the Senate vote on 18 May. The consensus
within the DFL was that it "would be a good thing, and should
have no opposition raised against it."[53] Nevertheless, there was
open dissension within the DFL. Richard Kroon, a delegate to
the DFL from the communist Painters' Union No. 37, led an
expected attack.[54] Others like Charles Bartlett were more
influentially placed to fight Martel on the issue. The treasurer
of an Electrical Workers' Union local in Detroit and a member
of the DFL legislative committee, Bartlett was also a five-term
representative from the First District of Wayne County and one
of nine members of the House to vote against the registration
law.[55]

---

[51] For example, " 'Open Shop' Bosses Lure Out-of-Town Labor to Detroit,"
Detroit Labor News, 26 September 1930, p. 1.

[52] "Selfish Interests Try to Thwart Relief of Jobless," *Detroit Labor News*,
14 November 1930, pp. 1, 2; "Unemployment Committee Asks Commuters Be
Stopped," *Detroit Labor News*, 28 November 1930, p. 1. Sidney Fine briefly
examines this particular conflict between employers' representatives and
unionists in his *Frank Murphy: The Detroit Years* (Ann Arbor: University of
Michigan Press, 1975), 288.

[53] "Labor Delegates Approve Bill to Register Aliens. Believe Measure Will
do Much to Prevent Bootlegging of Cheap Labor into Country," *Detroit Labor
News*, 22 May 1931, p. 1.

[54] Minutes of the DFL, 3 June 1931, Box 10, AFL-CIO Collection. Kroon
"brought more Communism into the ranks and locals of the American
Federation of Labor than any other Red," according to "A Survey of
Communist Activities in the City of Detroit and Vicinity," 1 July 1936, p. 4,
Communist Party, Box 1, AFL-CIO Collection.

[55] *State of Michigan, Official Directory and Legislative Manual, 1931-1932*
(Lansing: State of Michigan, 1931). Like Bartlett and many other members of
the DFL, Martel was also a Republican. He was a member of the GOP
District Committee and typically chaired the Resolutions Committee at the
party's Wayne County conventions. Martel subsequently became a Democrat

An "overwhelming majority" of the DFL stuck with Martel. They believed that alien registration would strengthen the enforcement of the nation's immigration laws which earlier "entangling and bewildering laws, regulations, orders, mandates and rulings" had emasculated. The unionists were not aware of, or did not concern themselves with, the repressive dimensions of the Spolansky Act which so agitated liberals, radicals, and immigrant leaders. The defense of wage and job standards in the labor market was vastly more important to them than worrying about aliens who might suffer hardships under the law. The registration law was of tremendous benefit to American workers, the DFL thought, because it would place innumerable obstacles in the way of commuting from Canada and in what Martel called "the trafficking among aliens by cheap-wage employers."[56]

That employers' groups opposed the law was another compelling reason for the majority of the DFL to support Martel. The irony of employers' opposition was that while liberals and radicals typically characterized the Union League of Michigan as a "reactionary group controlled by open-shop employers," the latter apparently lost control of the organization during the anti-communist drive of 1930-31.[57] Taking advantage of public disapproval of radicalism and hostility toward the constitutional rights of aliens, determined anti-communists within the Union League composed a registration law containing an employer sanctions clause which made it a misdemeanor to hire an alien who did not have a certificate of legal residence.[58] John Lovett, general manager of the Michigan Manufacturers Association, pointed to additional

---

when, in 1934, he was thrown out of the county convention for endorsing the Democratic state ticket. See Stephan B. and Vera H. Sarasohn, *Political Party Patterns in Michigan* (Detroit: Wayne State University Press, 1957), 27-28, 48-49.

[56] *Detroit Labor News*, 6 March, pp. 1, 4; and 5 June 1931, p. 1. According to attorney Theodore Levin, an opponent of the law, "The alien commuter who daily comes to work here from Canada would lose his standing. The commuter has his legal residence in Canada. . . . It is an injustice to the alien commuter who has complied with our Federal laws to suddenly find himself without a job. . . ." See the *Detroit News*, 31 May 1931, p. 2.

[57] This characterization appears in American Civil Liberties Union, *Annual Report of 1931-1932*, p. 31.

[58] Section 12, Michigan Public Act No. 241 of 1931.

problems with the law. He explained that employers would not always know when to ask prospective employees for proof of legal residence since it was difficult to tell the difference between aliens, particularly Canadians, and American citizens. Employers also did not relish taking on the burden of paperwork involved in enforcing the controversial law. Nor did employers welcome the state's interference in the labor market, according to Fred M. Butzel, a prominent liberal attorney who represented some unnamed Detroit manufacturers. His clients opposed the law because many of their highly skilled alien employees planned to resign rather than submit to registration and fingerprinting. In the press Butzel went on to defend freedom of movement and liberty of contract and upheld the labor-market status quo, suggesting that while "a great deal can be said in favor of a stable and settled population, it may be just as desirable to have a mobile force of labor that can come and go as needed"—certainly a bitter dose to take for Depression-era workers.[59]

For their part, Detroit communists brought together a highly vocal opposition to the Spolansky Act. Undoubtedly local communists also were surprised when Michigan passed an alien registration law, for the progress of the Fish Committee had led them to expect one out of Congress.[60] The issue of registration was nothing new to them. In 1928, they had assembled 70 representatives from 150 labor and fraternal groups under the auspices of the Detroit Council for the Protection of the Foreign Born to denounce registration and deportation measures pending in Congress. At the conference, attorneys Fred Butzel and Maurice Sugar told how the bills would circumvent constitutional protections and subject the alien portion of the population to police administration. They cautioned that registration would mark the first step toward the development of a nationwide passport and blacklist system.

---

[59] *Detroit News*, 30 May, p. 2 and 1 June 1931, p. 27; *Detroit Times*, 30 May 1931, p. 3.

[60] For examples, see the following: Provisional Committee for the Protection of the Foreign Born, Detroit, to all Working Class Organizations, October 1930, in Communism, Box 1, AFL-CIO Collection; Phil Raymond for State Senate, election flyer, January 1931, in Communist File, 1931, Box 2, Detroit Mayors' Papers, Burton Historical Collection, (hereafter BHC) Detroit Public Library, Detroit, Michigan.

And they emphasized that anti-alien legislation would equip employers with a club that they could use against workers who dared resist wage cuts and bad working conditions.[61]

The communists of Detroit echoed these and other themes in 1931 in preparation for a June 19th mass rally and protest demonstration featuring local and national speakers. They singled out for special condemnation Frank Martel and "the fascist leaders of the AFL [who] are helping the bosses," and warned that the registration law constituted a serious threat to all workers and not only aliens. Their main salvos hit the capitalists. In their flyers, communists labeled the Spolansky Act "the most vicious anti-labor, strike-breaking, terror measure, thus far devised by the enemies of the working class in the campaign to enforce the hunger and wage-cutting policies of the American ruling class." They dismissed as a ruse Governor Brucker's statement that the law would eliminate "undesirable aliens" and liberate scarce jobs for unemployed citizens. In reality, capitalists sought to use blacklisting and the threat of deportation against the foreign-born majority of the working class in order to build up the "tremendous reserve army" and restructure the labor market. "The sponsors and backers of the bill desire to create an army of outlaws in order to provide employers with an army of hounded scabs and strikebreakers, who will be forced, under the threat of deportation, to take jobs during strikes and slave at any price, without struggle or resistance. Workers who will refuse to be herded like cattle and serve as scabs will simply be branded 'undesirable' and deported at the will of the bosses."[62]

To help build and pay for their June 19th demonstration, the communists made overtures to sympathizers and liberals. But many liberals did not require communist prompting to enter the fray. Some like Fred Butzel and Detroit Mayor Frank Murphy were unusually sensitive to the rights of immigrants as a barometer of the liberties of citizens.[63] Other liberals, such

---

[61] *The Autoworkers News*, May 1928, p. 3.

[62] Flyers for the 19 June 1931 events appear in Communism, Box 1, AFL-CIO Collection. According to the press, 2,000 people assembled for the demonstration at Grand Circus Park and 3,500 for the mass meeting at Olympia Arena—far short of the hoped for 100,000. See the *Detroit News*, 20 June 1931, p. 5.

[63] Fred M. Butzel, Reading Room File, BHC; *Detroit News*, 1 June 1931, p. 27; Fine, *Frank Murphy*, 178-79.

as recently elected state Senator George Sadowski, emphasized the danger to workers. Sadowski, based in Detroit's east-side wards and the first Democratic senator in Lansing in some sixteen years, declared in a letter to the *Detroit News* that, "the main purpose for this bill is to strike a blow upon the laboring class in Michigan—regardless whether they be citizens or aliens." Although unmindful of organized labor's endorsment of the law, Sadowski nevertheless predicted that the Spolansky Act would "boomerang politically" on Republicans in 1932. "The Republican administration," he charged, "has already gone far enough in protecting the property rights of industry and big business. It is high time that labor receives some consideration of their personal rights."[64]

Probably most crucial in the ranks of the opposition was the Detroit branch of the American Civil Liberties Union. The ACLU saw the Spolansky Act as part of a threatening pattern of reactionary legislation descending across the country, from loyalty oaths for teachers and the curtailment of worker's First Amendment rights during strikes to censorship and illegal arrests of aliens.[65] In early 1931, members of the local branch had expected the recommendations of the Fish Committee to generate repressive legislation in Congress, not Lansing. But right after the Senate vote they began to map their legal strategy. Initially the ACLU tried to convince Governor Brucker not to sign the bill, advising that it was not needed since existing criminal laws were strong enough to handle any conspiracy to overthrow the government, that it discriminated against aliens, and that it would lead to the registration of the entire population. Moreover, they pointed out that the bill was unconstitutional as it represented blatant state interference with the federal government's absolute jurisdiction over immigration.[66]

For a moment Brucker wavered. His hestitation probably has little to do with the ACLU's protests or the militancy of the communists. Rather, Attorney General Paul W. Voorheis believed that the bill was unconstitutional and he tried to

---

[64] George G. Sadowski, Reading Room File, BHC; Sarasohn, *Political Party Patterns in Michigan*, 24; *Detroit News*, 31 May 1931, p. 10.

[65] ACLU, *Monthly Bulletin for Action*, June 1931, Reel 3.

[66] *Detroit Times*, 20 May 1931, p. 1; *Detroit News*, 26 May, p. 31 and 28 May 1931, p. 13; ACLU, *Weekly Press Bulletin*, 21 May 1931, Reel 3.

prevent Brucker from signing by refusing to issue a legal opinion. More seriously, Brucker worried about opposition from manufacturers. He agreed to sign the bill on 29 May only when his close ally, Assistant Attorney General Kit W. Clardy, advised that the employer sanctions provision was invalid and, therefore, would not inconvience business interests. Clardy assured the governor that enough of the law would survive legal challenges, especially the registration sections, to still make it work. The director of immigration for the Detroit district, John L. Zurbrick, who welcomed the act as a supplement to federal immigration law, similarly placated Brucker's worries about the constitutional status of the act.[67]

Opponents quickly pounced on the Spolansky Act. On 1 June, attorneys for the ACLU sued the state in federal district court on behalf of George Arrowsmith, a British immigrant and construction employer, and obtained an order blocking enforcement of the law. The next day state officials began dismantling their preparations to register aliens.[68] In less than a week after becoming the law the Spolansky Act was practically dead. Legally the act lingered until early December when a panel of three federal judges in the case of *Arrowsmith v. Voorheis* rejected the state's defense that the act represented a legitimate exercise of its police powers and, instead, ruled it unconstitutional on the grounds that it usurped the authority of the federal government relative to the control of immigration and the disposition of aliens. The court's decision was inherently conservative. In effect, it rejected the State of Michigan's claim of overriding political necessity and its right to interfere with the nationwide movement and employment of free wage labor. Although the court did not rule on the constitutionality of alien registration per se, the state never appealed the decision, and a year later one of the ACLU attorneys, Attorney General-elect Patrick O'Brien, secured a permanent injunction against enforcement of the law.[69]

The rapid demise of the Spolansky Act dimmed the hopes of the DFL and anti-communists that they could do battle with

---

[67] Sugar, "Michigan Passes the 'Spolansky Act'," 33; *Detroit News*, 28 May, p. 13; 30 May, p. 2; and 1 June 1931, p. 27.

[68] *Detroit News*, 1 June, pp. 1, 27; and 2 June 1931, p. 12.

[69] *Arrowsmith v. Voorheis*, 55 F.(2d)310 (E.D. Mich. 1931); *Detroit News*, 9 December 1931, pp. 1-2; *New York Times*, 20 December 1932.

cheap foreign labor and communist subversion by passing immigration and anti-alien laws through the state legislature. The strategy inevitably would fail so long as federal courts upheld the integrity of the national labor market, which they had done time after time since 1876, and as they did again in *Arrowsmith v. Voorheis.*[70] But this was hardly the end of anti-communism or Jacob Spolansky. In 1932-33, Spolansky struck back when he secured the arrest and deportation of Tony Antonoff, the Bulgarian-born communist who had built the 19 June 1931, demonstration against the alien registration bill.[71] Throughout the remainder of the 1930s Spolansky remained close to conservative circles, advised Chrysler Corporation on plant security matters, served as deputy sheriff in the Wayne County Sheriff's office, and in 1938 testified before the House Un-American Activities Committee when it came to Detroit looking into communist infiltration in the revived labor movement.[72]

Nor did the failure of the Spolansky Act end nativism and attempts at government management of American politics through tough immigration laws and alien registration. In 1940, a Congress worried about German fifth columnists and communist subversion of the military passed the nation's first compulsory alien registration law. And as debate over employer sanctions in the Federal Immigration Reform and Control Act of 1986 demonstrated, the contest between organized labor and employers for control of the American labor market was far from over in 1931.

---

[70] Benjamin J. Klebaner, "State and Local Immigration Regulation in the United States Before 1882," *International Review of Social History* 3 (1958): 287.

[71] Minutes of Executive Committee of Council for Protection of Foreign Born, 3 June 1931, in Communism, Box 1, AFL-CIO; *Michigan Worker,* 6 November 1932, p. 1; "A Survey of Communist Activities in the City of Detroit and Vicinity," 9. Spolansky's involvement in the arrest of Antoff led to speculation that he was the target of assassination by the communists. See Office of Prosecuting Attorney of Wayne County to Maj. Gen. George Van Horn Moseley, Deputy Chief of Staff, U.S. Army, 10 August 1932, *U.S. Military Intelligence Reports: Surveillance of Radicals in the United States, 1917-1941* (Frederick, Md.: University Publications of America, 1985), Reel 23.

[72] Spolansky, *The Communist Trail,* Chapter 4.

Class, Craft, and Culture:
Tool and Die Makers and the
Organization of the UAW

by
Steve Babson

As though they were one man the workers of Detroit got in
motion . . . . all in one mass, men and women, Negro and
white, all together . . . .

The *United Auto Worker*, national newspaper of the fledgling
UAW, projected this stirring image of worker militancy in
1937. The tone of the passage is inspirational, the perspective
is militantly class-bound, and the myth is enduring: the sit-
down strikes and organizing drives of the 1930s, we are told,
were majoritarian and spontaneous. Popular histories abound
with this imagery, much of it originating with participants and
reported subsequently by journalists, partisans, and finally,
some historians.[1]

There is an opposing vision of the 1930s labor movement that
turns this popular myth inside out. Articulated by some
participants and by a growing number of labor historians, this
contrary perspective focuses on the role of an activist minority
in sparking the mass actions of the 1930s. Instead of a
spontaneous and unified rank and file, it stresses the uneven
development of militancy, the calculation and hesitancy of the

---

Steve Babson is employed by the Wayne State Labor Studies Center and is a
Ph.D. candidate in labor history at Wayne State University.

[1] The *United Auto Worker* passage was quoted in Mary Heaton Vorse,
Labor's New Millions (New York: New Age Books, 1938), 92. Worker
"spontaneity" is invoked by Jeremy Brecher, *Strike!* (San Francisco: Straight
Arrow, 1972), 233-236 and passim, and by Art Preis, *Labor's Giant Step* (New
York: Pathfinder, 1972), 53-54 and 64-65, as a club to punish, in Preis' words,
those "abject servants of the capitalistic class," union officials; by Richard
Boyer and Herbert Morais, *Labor's Untold Story* (New York: United Electrical
Workers, 1955), 290-291, to exalt the heroism of the sit-downers; and by James
Green, *The World of the Worker: Labor in Twentieth Century America* (New
York: Hill and Wang, 1980), 155; and David Brody, *Workers in Industrial
America: Essays on the Twentieth Century Struggle* (New York: Oxford
University Press, 1980), 103, in lieu of an adequate concept of leadership that
encompasses more than just the union's national executive board.

Michigan Historical Review 14 (Spring 1988)

majority of workers, and the initiating role played by strategic groups.[2]

This essay falls within the second perspective. In examining the growth of auto worker unionism in Detroit during the 1930s, I will focus on the dynamics of craft, class, and culture that propelled two overlapping groups, skilled tool and die makers and Anglo-Irish immigrants, into prominent leadership roles within the UAW. There is, of course, something paradoxical in these two numerically insignificant groups taking leadership in an industry where semiskilled labor was the norm and where East Europeans were the predominant immigrant group. Yet, however incongruous, tool and die makers and the Anglo-Irish stand out like colored yarn in the warp and weave of the UAW's organizational history.

The initiating role of tool and die makers is especially visible. It was 500 tool and die makers in the Vernor Avenue plant of Briggs Manufacturing who, by successfully striking against a wage cut in January 1933, inspired a multi-employer walkout of 15,000 production workers—the first mass strike in the history of Detroit's auto industry.[3]

It was tool and die makers who, in the fall of 1933, established the Mechanics' Educational Society of America as the first auto union to successfully strike and negotiate on an industry-wide basis. It was the UAW's East Side Tool and Die Local 155, formed by former MESA activists, that organized and led Detroit's first sit-down strike at Midland Steel in November 1936. And it was pro-CIO tool and die makers at General Motors who, by striking during model changeover in the summer of 1939, forced the industry's leading employer to recognize the UAW-CIO over the discredited UAW-AFL.[4]

---

[2] See Sidney Fine, *Sit-Down: The General Motors Strike of 1936-1937* (Ann Arbor: University of Michigan Press, 1969); Peter Freidlander, *The Emergence of a UAW Local, 1936-1939* (Pittsburgh: University of Pittsburgh Press, 1975); and Nelson Lichtenstein, "Auto Worker Militancy and the Structure of Factory Life, 1937-1955," *The Journal of American History* 67 (November 1980): 335-353.

[3] The initiating role of the Briggs tool and die workers strike is described by Phil Raymond, "The Briggs Auto Strike Victory," *Labor Unity* (March 1933): 21-24, Robert Dunn Collection, Box 3, Folder 3-23, Walter Reuther Archives, Wayne State University, Detroit, Michigan. Hereafter this collection will be cited as Reuther Archives, WSU.

[4] See (among others) Harry Dahlheimer, *A History of the Mechanics'*

The tool and die makers in this last strike were led by a Scotsman, Bill Stevenson, chairman of the negotiating committee, president of Detroit's West Side Tool and Die Local 157, and second only to Walter Reuther in devising the strategy that made the UAW-CIO victorious.[5] Another Scotsman, John Anderson, president of the East Side Tool and Die Local, was chief organizer of the pivotal Midland steel sit-down. And yet another Britisher, Matthew Smith, was the founding leader of the Mechanics' Educational Society, a union in which European-born workers were a majority and British workers were a plurality.

Many of Detroit's biggest factory locals also drew some portion of their leadership from the Anglo-Irish immigrants clustered in toolrooms and other skilled enclaves within the plants. Four of the first six presidents of the UAW's largest local, situated in the Ford Motor Company's massive Rouge plant, came from the British Isles: Bill McKie, a Scottish sheet-metal worker and president of the Ford Federal Local at its founding; W.G. Grant, a tool and die maker from England, elected president of the Rouge's Local 600 in 1944; Joe McCusker, a toolmaker and former coal miner from Lanarkshire, Scotland, elected local president in 1945 for the first of two terms; and Tommy Thompson, an Englishman and former coal miner, elected president in 1947. Even Thompson's opponent, the Irishman Michael Magee, came from the United Kingdom. So too did some of the early presidents of Packard Local 190, Cadillac Local 22, West Side Local 174, and Dodge Local 3. This last local was led by Pat Quinn, a former Irish Republican Army foot soldier and leading organizer of the Dodge sit-down strike—the biggest plant occupation in 1937 or any other year in American labor history.

In the 1930s and early 1940s there was hardly a UAW bargaining committee in Detroit that did not have at least one

---

Educational Society of America in Detroit (Detroit: Wayne State University Press, 1951); Steve Babson, *Working Detroit: The Making of a Union Town* (Detroit: Wayne State University Press, 1986), 51-110; and John Barnard, "Rebirth of the United Automobile Workers: The General Motors Tool and Diemakers' Strike of 1939," *Labor History* 27 (Spring 1986): 165-187.

[5] The summary account that follows of Anglo-Irish leadership in auto worker unions is drawn from my article "Pointing the Way: The Role of British and Irish Skilled Tradesmen in the Rise of the UAW," *Detroit in Perspective* 7 (Spring 1983): 75-96.

member who spoke with a brogue or a Yorkshire accent, or answered to the name "Scotty." At the other end of the scale, between 1935 and 1948, at least eight of the union's International Executive Board members were Scottish, Irish, or English. Leonard Woodcock, the union's fourth president, was born in Rhode Island but raised in Europe by his English parents; his father, a diemaker, brought the family to Detroit in 1928 and later became an early strike leader at the Motor Products Corporation. Doug Fraser, the union's fifth president, was born in Glasgow; his father, an electrician, was a strike leader in the DeSoto plant during the 1937 sit-down.

What brought these Anglo-Irish tradesmen to Detroit? And why did the tool and die makers among them play such a prominent leadership role in the rise of the UAW? The answer to both questions starts with a brief look at the nature of tool and die work and its relationship to production skills in auto manufacturing.

In the early years of the industry, skilled mechanics working alone or in teams assembled the entire car at stationary workplaces, using hand tools to file and hammer the ill-fitting parts into place. Standardized and interchangeable parts—the necessary prerequisites for assembly-line production—could not be produced by the craft methods employed in most machine shops before 1910. Machinists varied in their skills, attitudes, and performance on the job; and, therefore, the parts they produced on operator-controlled machines also varied in their approximation of the blueprinted design.[6]

Watch and gunmakers had already produced nearly interchangeable parts in the nineteenth century,[7] but achieving the same goal in carmaking was no easy matter. Even the

---

[6] See Allan Nevins, *Ford: The Times, The Man The Company* (New York: Charles Scribners Sons, 1954), 354-386; Stephen Meyer, *The Five Dollar Day: Labor Management and Social Control in the Ford Motor Company, 1908-1921* (Albany: State University of New York, 1981), 9-36; David Hounshell, *From the American System to Mass Production, 1800-1932* (Baltimore: John Hopkins, 1984), Chapter 6; Jack Russell, "The Coming of the Line," *Radical America* 12 (May-June 1978): 28-45; and Joyce Shaw Peterson, "Auto Workers and Their Work, 1900-1933," *Labor History* 22 (Spring 1981): 213-236.

[7] See Merritt Roe Smith, *Harpers Ferry Armory and the New Technology: The Challenge of Change* (Ithaca: Cornell University, 1977); David Landes, *Revolution in Time: Clocks and the Making of the Modern World* (Cambridge: Harvard University, 1983).

Courtesy of National Automotive History Collection, Detroit Public Library

Welding

(Welding "jigs" are visible in the door of this 1940 Buick. The jigs are precision-made clamps built by tool makers to hold the separate body sub-assemblies — roof, cowling, and frame — in perfect alignment for welding.)

simplest car was a far more complex machine than a watch or a gun. Yet the same principles applied. As in the older branches of metal working, the first step towards interchangeability was the use of specialized "jigs and fixtures" to situate and hold parts as they were machined and welded. Where before, the machine-tool operator fastened the work into the drill or lathe with moveable set screws and clamps, now a special fixture, using a cam or some other device, mechanically guided the part into place and held it firmly. Parts machined in this way could be produced with unerring precision: barring a malfunction, a well-designed fixture guided the machining process through the same path time after time.[8]

The growing use of stamping dies contributed even more decisively to the mass production of interchangeable parts. Metalworkers had long used simple dies to punch out uniform parts with cookie-cutter precision, and automakers quickly adopted the process to produce small parts like clips, braces, and brackets. But as they searched for alternatives to the heavy castings then in use for larger parts, they developed increasingly elaborate dies to stamp out axle housings, frames, brake drums, crank cases, and especially body panels. The stampings were not only lighter than cast-metal parts, but, as the *American Machinist* noted, "many machining operations were eliminated and parts were delivered to the plant ready for assembly."[9] By the 1920s, stamping dies were the key technology in many areas of auto parts manufacturing. "In fact," observed *Chrysler Motors Magazine* in a 1935 article, " 'Always say Die' might be accepted as a cardinal principle of the industry."[10]

---

[8] "The tedious cut-and-try lapping method of final finishing is now a thing of the dark ages of automobile building. Gears are machined, hardened and made ready for use without any running in being necessary. By the use of special machines and small tool devices—jigs, fixtures and others—parts are now produced more quickly and cheaply than ever before and with complete interchangeability." "Influence of the Automobile on Machine Tool Design," *American Machinist* 44 (13 January 1916): 82.

[9] W.W. Galbreath and John Winter, "Development of Modern Stamping Practice," *American Machinist* 59 (13 December 1923): 885. See also "Pressed Steel Automobile Parts," *Horseless Age* 14 (8 September 1909): 263-264; Mortier LaFever, "Workers, Machinery, and Production in the Automobile Industry," *Monthly Labor Review* 19 (October 1924): 749-750.

[10] Royal Rusell, "Split the Line," *Chrysler Motors Magazine* 2 (September 1935): 5.

The use of dies and special tools had at least as great an impact on the distribution of skills in auto manufacturing as the more celebrated moving assembly line. The assembly line, after all, was only feasible once stamping dies and machine-tool fixtures made it possible to mass produce interchangeable parts that required little or no fitting in assembly.[11] Skilled production workers, bench hands, molders, sheet metal workers, and woodworkers could be replaced with less skilled assemblers and machine operators. "Very few skilled workmen were necessary," as one Ford stockholder report noted in 1913, "except in the tool room."[12]

And here was the critical issue for automakers seeking to remove "all possible brain work," as Frederick Taylor recommended, from the shop to the planning department. A considerable amount of brain work could indeed be removed from production crafts to the planning department, but before the mechanized instruments of management control could be installed (in lieu of "brains") on the shop floor, the planning department would have to turn to a troublesome intermediary: the tool and die maker.

Blanche Bernstein, in her labor market studies for the Works Progress Administration, aptly summarized the process. Skill, she wrote in 1937, rather than being removed from the shop floor, "has been shifted and restricted to the preparation of tool and dies."[13] Demand for the highly skilled workers who prepared these tools grew accordingly. As early as 1910, the *American Machinist* reported that tool and die makers arriving

---

[11] "The use of steel stampings has been one of the greatest factors in body progress . . . . Stampings come from the press uniform in contour and size and consequently modern body production output has been based on this uniformity of the metal sheets as they are received from the stamping department. In fact . . . no single factor is so important as the use of metal stampings, and in proportion as the volume will permit the absorption of the die cost, the final cost of the body can be reduced." George Mercer, "Standard Bodies Are Now Produced at One-Third Pre-War Cost," *Automotive Industries* 53 (24 September 1925): 494.

[12] United States Board of Tax Appeals, "Petitioners Statement of Facts," 18 April 1927, 76-77, Dodge Estate, Legal, Asscession 96, Box 7, Ford Archives, Henry Ford Museum, Dearborn, Michigan.

[13] Blanche Bernstein, "Labor Market in the Auto Industry, 1937," *Reemployment Opportunities and Recent Changes in Industrial Techniques,* (Washington, D.C.: Works Progress Administration, 1937), 24, in Chalmers Collection, Box 2, Reuther Archives, WSU.

in Detroit from all over the country had to be temporarily housed in tents.[14] Seventeen years later, Henry Ford employed 227 tool designers and 17,000 tool room workers to prepare the Rouge plant for the Model A.[15] Industry-wide, even as the percentage of skilled bench workers, machine-tool operators and sheet metal workers declined during the 1920s, the proportion of tool and die makers rose.[16]

Finding these skilled workers was no easy task, especially since the very process that produced a growing demand for tool and die makers also reduced the supply of these vital craftsmen. Tools and dies made it possible to dilute production skills and pigeon-hole workers into ever more specialized tasks. But by producing, as one writer in the *American Machinist* put it, "more half-baked mechanics than any other country in the world," this same strategy of specialization also undermined apprenticeship and restricted the long-term supply of tool and die makers who made such specialization possible.[17]

A few employers, notably Ford and, to a lessor extent, General Motors, established trade schools to augment their supply of skilled machinists. Most companies did not bother. Training was expensive and there was no guarantee that journeymen would stay with a company once their apprenticeship ended. Poaching was cheaper in any case. As *Automotive Industries* observed in 1925, most employers had "an attitude of extreme apathy towards the question of training skilled workers . . . . Production men in general seem to be content to hire those men who have been trained by other industries."[18]

Of course such poaching, however rational for the individual firm, only aggravated the industry-wide problem by bidding up the cost of toolroom workers. There was, however, another source of skilled labor that increased overall supply without costly training programs. That source was Europe.

---

[14] C.B. Gordy, "Craftsmen Needed," *American Machinist* 79 (6 November 1935): 823.

[15] Allan Nevins and Frank Hill, *Ford: Expansion and Challenge* (New York: Charles Scribners Sons, 1957), 451.

[16] Bernstein, "Labor Market in the Auto Industry," 34.

[17] William Peterson, "Wanted: Broader Training," *American Machinist* 79 (9 October 1935): 749.

[18] Norman Shidle, "Automotive Factory Labor Costs Cut 10-50 Percent in Last Two Years," *Automotive Industries* 53 (10 September 1925): 402.

Twentieth century emigration from Europe to North America is not often associated with skilled workers from the British Isles—Great Britain is presumed to have already sent its "Birds of Passage" on the wing before 1900.[19] In fact, heavy emigration from Britain revived in the decade before World War I, especially in the years 1908-1910 when net emigration to North America surpassed 370,000 people.[20] At the time, Americans preoccupied with a surge of immigration from eastern and southern Europe overlooked the half million British arriving in the United States between 1905 and 1912.[21] Today, historians of North American immigration compound this blind spot by overlooking emigration to Canada, the favored destination for the English after 1905 and the Scots after 1907.[22] Following World War I, British emigration continued at high levels, with a net outflow from the United Kingdom of more than one million people in the 1920s.[23]

Of those arriving in the United States, upwards of 40 percent were skilled workers, a proportion that topped all other immigrant groups.[24] The high wages and plentiful job openings of America's booming economy beckoned from across the Atlantic, and the British economy, stagnant before World War

---

[19] See Michael Piore, *Birds of Passage: Migrant Labor and Industrial Societies* (Cambridge: Cambridge University Press, 1979), 141-166.

[20] Stanley Johnson, *A History of Immigration from the United Kingdom to North America* (London: Routledge, 1913), 344-347.

[21] *Historical Statistics of the United States, Colonial Times to 1970, Part I*, United States Department of Commerce, Bureau of the Census, Series C 89-119, 105.

[22] Rowland T. Berthoff, *British Immigrants in Industrial America* (Cambridge: Harvard University, 1953), 21.

[23] R.S. Walshaw, *Migration To and From the British Isles* (London: Jonathan Cape Ltd., 1941), 13-14.

[24] Clifton Yearly Jr., *Britons in American Labor* (Baltimore: John Hopkins University, 1957), 20-21. Yearly's figures cover the period 1873-1918. Available evidence suggests a comparable proportion of British immigrants in the 1920s were also skilled. In 1923, the American Consul in Manchester reported that 5,815 people departed from the Manchester consular district in the twelve months following 1 July 1922, of whom 1,018 were textile workers, 1,113 were skilled workers, 765 were "domestics, housewives, and servants," 371 were coal miners, 287 were professionals, 247 were unskilled laborers, and 1,142 were unidentified. Most of the latter were wives and children, and many of the textile workers and coal miners were skilled or semi-skilled. See "Emigration from the Manchester Consular District During the Period 7/1/22 to 6/30/23," National Archives, 53531/52, Emigration England: Canada: 1924.

I and severely depressed in the 1920s, gave many an unemployed worker an added push. A significant minority of emigrant tradesmen had also been blacklisted by employers in the years of peak strike activity between the engineers' lockout of 1922 and the General Strike of 1926.

Detroit auto companies paid premium wages for these workers, many of whom possessed the finely honed skills that specialization had eliminated or diluted in United States production operations. Since Europe lagged well behind America in developing a mass market, "toolroom" methods still prevailed in many of Britain's metalworking factories, and a larger proportion of the mechanics trained in this craft-oriented environment could still lay out and perform precision work, including die and fixture making.[25] The exact number of British workers in Detroit's toolrooms is difficult to measure, but most sources agree that the majority of toolroom workers in the 1920s and 1930s were foreign born, and that the British were the most prominent among them. They were closely followed by German machinists who also emigrated to Detroit in large numbers during the 1920s.[26]

This ready source of skilled labor was sharply curtailed, however, when the economic doldrums that gripped Europe for most of the 1920s finally overcame the United States. After 1929, immigration from the British Isles tailed off to insignificant levels, and the few employers who trained homegrown mechanics dropped their apprenticeship programs.

---

[25] The British car industry did not begin to "rationalize" production on the American model until after World War II; between 1948 and 1959, car production soared 180 percent. Production at Ford's Dagenham plant rose from 400,000 vehicles in 1946 to 1.4 million in 1955. See Huw Beynon, *Working for Ford* (London: Allen Lane, 1973), 45-46.

[26] W.E. Chalmers, a close observer of Detroit's auto industry in the 1920s and 1930s, estimated that a majority of Detroit's job-shop tool and die makers in 1933 came from Germany, Scotland, and England. See "First Strikes in the Automobile Industry," IV-2, typescript, W.E. Chalmers Collection, Box 8, Folder 8-3, Reuther Archives, WSU. Bill Stevenson, president of the UAW's West Side Tool and Die Local 157, estimated that 70 percent of the industry's tool and die makers were born in Europe. See Oral History Interview of Bill Stevenson, p. 6, Reuther Archives, WSU. Of the 499 tool and die makers employed at the Vernor Avenue plant of Briggs Manufacturing in August 1930, 61 percent were foreign born. See "Table 1: Data Regarding Representative Groups of Tool and Die Makers," #2, in the Joe Brown Collection, Box 15, Folder "MESA," Reuther Archives, WSU.

Despite employer efforts to minimize their reliance on skilled tool and die makers, principally by fragmenting certain elements of toolroom work and by using duplicate dies for several different body styles, the auto industry faced a critical shortage of these skilled workers when sales and production began to revive in 1935. "This shortage is marked," the *American Machinist* warned, "especially in these past few months during the peak of preparation for 1936 models."[27]

As noted earlier, tool and die makers played a disproportionately large role in the organizing activity that peaked in Detroit during 1936-1939. The evolution of automotive technology had put these workers in a strategic position within the industry, and the developing shortage of their vital skills gave them added bargaining leverage with their employers. But there was no technological imperative behind their successful leadership of the UAW. Before 1929, tool and die makers more often allied themselves with the narrow craft tradition of the AFL or spurned organization altogether.

Indeed, the pre-depression tool and die maker was a close approximation of the "labor aristocrat" vilified in Leninist theory. The toolmaker's strategic position in the industry won him the highest wages and the most privileged status in the blue collar workforce. And in a world that ranked white Anglo-Saxon men well above women, minorities, and ethnics, the toolroom workforce stood out as predominantely northern European and exclusively white and male.[28]

The toolroom was also a seedbed of entrepreneurial talent. Virtually all of the industry's pioneer automakers began as machinists, many of them learning the trade in family-owned blacksmith shops—the Dodge Brothers, Ransom Olds—or as machine-shop apprentices—David Buick, Walter Chrysler,

---

[27] C.B. Gordy, "Craftsmen Needed," 823.

[28] Black workers could generally find auto industry jobs in those occupations that white workers shunned—principally in foundries, paint spraying departments, and janitorial work. See August Meier and Elliot Rudwick, *Black Detroit and the Rise of the UAW* (New York: Oxford University Press, 1979), 7-8. Women workers were concentrated in small parts fabrication and upholstery sewing; immigrant Poles, Italians, and other ethnic groups from southern and eastern Europe predominated in production departments. See Steve Babson, *Working Detroit,* 17-50.

Henry Ford, and Henry Leland.[29] By the 1920s, few tool and die makers could hope to reproduce the meteoric rise of these early pioneers, but the stunning elaboration of die and machine-tool designs in the 1910s and 1920s allowed many enterprising tradesmen to open small job shops producing die components and precision tooling for the auto industry.[30] Others could cross the threshold into white-collar, managerial status by becoming tool designers or plant managers; the contrast with the negligible entreprenuerial opportunities of semi-skilled machine operators and assembly-line workers is obvious.[31]

The contrast extended to living conditions. "In 1929 . . . many skilled workers income ran [to] $2,340," recalled Scotsman Bill McKie, testifying before the Henderson Committee hearings of 1934. "Houses were built, the installment man was busy on the job, we were all buying radios, we were all buying cars." With annual earnings nearly 50 percent higher than production workers, "these men," McKie continued, "attempted to invest their earning in the buying of lots and homes and all kinds of appliances to help their wives at home, such as washing machines and things of this description."[32] The steadily growing proportion of women auto workers in production operations belied the "wife at home" ideal of middle-class respectability, but the machine shop was still 98 percent male when the United States Bureau of Labor Statistics surveyed the industry in 1928.[33]

Their privileged and prosperous status made tool and die makers one of the least militant groups in the auto industry

---

[29] See George May, *A Most Unique Machine: The Michigan Origins of the American Automobile Industry* (Grand Rapids, Mich.: William B. Eerdmans Publishing, 1975).

[30] The tool and die industry was in this respect comparable to the contemporary computer software industry.

[31] At Ford, examples include Joseph Galamb, the Hungarian-born head of the company's engineering department, Carl Johansson, the Swedish-born inventor of "Jo" Blocks, and John Findlater, the Scottish-born head of pressed steel operations, all of whom worked for varying lengths of time as journeymen tool and die makers before coming to Ford. Charles Sorensen, the Danish-born production manager at the Rouge plant, had worked as a journeyman pattern maker and served as secretary of Detroit's Pattern Makers' union before coming to Ford.

[32] McKie's testimony was quoted in *New Masses* (8 January 1935), 16-17, Joe Brown Scrapbook, Volume 3, Reuther Archives, WSU.

[33] *Federated Press*, 23 March 1928, 2.

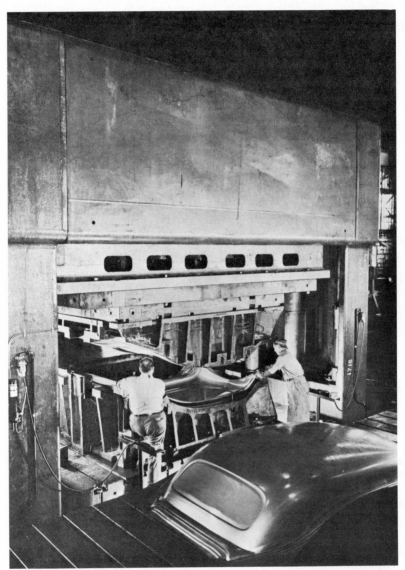

Stamping Roof Panels in a Fisher Body Plant

(Construction of these enormous stamping dies required the highest degree of skill.)

before 1929. Quickie strikes and departmental walkouts frequently disrupted production during the 1920s, but most of these job actions were concentrated in production departments and particularly in body making, where metal finishers, trimmers, and upholsterers confronted technological change and piece-work cuts.[34] The left-wing Auto Workers Union appealed to these semi-skilled groups, not to tool and die makers, when it tried to build plant organizations during the 1920s. And even these semi-skilled workers still clung to craft identities that undermined a class alliance with their less-skilled co-workers. "They wanted to build a fence around themselves," said Nick DiGaetano of the metal finishers at Chrysler in the late 1920s. "The foundry men? 'Hell with them,' they said. The assembly-line men? 'Hell with them, they have no trade,' they said. The polisher [metal finisher] was a big shot, like the molder, like the machinist, like the tool maker . . . ."[35]

Needless to say, it was the depression that deflated this cock-sure attitude and motivated these downwardly mobile craftsmen to take action. The outlines of that disaster and its general impact on autoworkers is well known. We need only focus here on two aspects of the crisis that hit tool and die makers especially hard. The first was the introduction of "inside contracting" as a management technique for driving down toolroom wages. In a cruel twist of the entrepreneurial dynamic that characterized the 1920s, job shop employers after 1929 began to put die making jobs up for competitive bidding within the shop: the worker who bid the lowest number of hours to complete the job got the work. Since workers desperate for employment routinely low-balled their bids, diemaker wages plunged from pre-1929 rates of $1 or more an hour to an

---

[34] UAW editor Henry Kraus obtained (probably from Phil Raymond) a list of twenty-six departmental walkouts that occurred between 1926 and 1929—only one involved tool and die makers. See "Record of Struggles," Henry Kraus Collection, Box 1, Folder "Auto Workers Union—Causes and Results of Work Stoppages, April 1926-May 1929," Reuther Archives, WSU. W.E. Chalmers compiled a similar list of eleven walkouts occurring between 1918 and 1929—none included tool and die makers. See W.E. Chalmers, "Labor in the Automobile Industry: A Study of Personnel Policies, Workers Attitudes, and Attempts at Unionism" (Ph.D. diss., University of Wisconsin, 1932), 208-212.

[35] Oral History Interview, Nick DiGaetano, 50, Reuther Archives, WSU.

effective rate in some job shops of 25 cents an hour by 1933—
lower than some production worker wages.[36]

The 1933 tool and die makers' strike led by the Mechanics'
Educational Society of America eliminated inside contracting
and halted wholesale wage cutting. But MESA could not
eliminate a second problem that confronted tool and die
makers: seasonal work. An industry-wide characteristic of auto
employment before the 1930s, seasonality had always been
especially pronounced for tool and die makers. In the 1920s,
they often worked only seven months a year preparing tools
and dies for the upcoming production season, but high wages
and heavy overtime had produced high annual earnings. In the
early 1930s, production cutbacks and a sharp curtailment of die
programs pared the work season down to four months and less
for many tool and die makers. "They have lost their homes,
have had their automobiles repossessed, their furniture
mortgaged," MESA leader Matthew Smith said of fellow
tradesmen who could not find enough work in 1934: "To eke
out an existence, these men, the 'aristocracy of automobile
labor,' arrange to go on welfare, try door-to-door selling, or
plead for odd jobs."[37]

Some tool and die makers, in short, fell further and harder
than many production workers.[38] In this respect, the depression
acted as a great leveler, pulling down the "fences" that

---

[36] On inside contracting and wages of tool and die makers, see Henry
Dahlheimer, *A History of the Mechanics Educational Society,* 2; Joe Brown,
"The MESA: Tool and Die Makers Organize and Strike," typescript, p. 3, in the
Joe Brown Collection, Box 23, Folder "Strikes, Tool and Die, 1933," Reuther
Archives, WSU; Matthew Smith, General Secretary of the Mechanics
Educational Society of America, Before the President's Commission of Inquiry
into Conditions in the Automobile Industry, Detroit, Michigan, 12/16/34," p. 2,
Joe Brown Collection, Box 17, Folder "NRA—Decisions and Orders," Reuther
Archives, WSU. Wage comparisons between production and skilled workers in
1933 are difficult, since nominal wage rates did not reflect actual pay for either
group—skilled workers, as noted, low-balled their bids for inside contracts and
therefore worked many hours without pay, while production workers on group
incentive bonuses lost pay for down time. Average 1933 hourly earnings in the
auto industry (before the NIRA code) were 58.6 cents. See "Memorandum to
Mr. Sidney Hillman, National Industrial Recovery Board," 23 October 1934
from the Labor Advisory Board, p. 2, in Chalmers Collection, Box 2, Folder
"U.S. Auto Labor Board, Correspondence, 8/34-12/34," Reuther Archives, WSU.

[37] Smith, "A Statement of Mathew Smith," 2.

[38] Experience varied widely, however. Some tool and die makers I have
interviewed were never laid off in the 1930s. It happens that among those I

separated skilled and less skilled workers. No longer able to earn the family wage that sustained the wife as a full-time homemaker, the underemployed tool and die worker postponed marriage or, if already married, confronted the possibility his wife might have to seek wage-work. In the meantime, MESA, discovering it could not effectively close a plant when nonstriking production workers crossed their lines, opened its ranks to the many women operating punch presses in larger job shops and auto plants. The economic crisis affected family and gender relations as well as material conditions, and it was in this context that the UAW's East Side Tool and Die Local 155 established Detroit's first Women's Auxiliary during the Midland Steel sit-down of November 1936—with membership initially open to both wives and women workers.[39]

The foreign-born tool and die makers who led this strike and played such a crucial role in organizing the UAW were well suited to leadership. Europe's metalworkers, especially in Britain and Germany, had established sizeable unions and a growing political presence before World War I. A significant minority had gone beyond the moderate agenda of Labour Party and Social Democratic politics and joined the revolutionary left, and the organizational skills these activists possessed were an invaluable resource for the fledgling UAW. British and Irish tradesmen were especially prominent in these regards: as former citizens of the United Kingdom, they possessed a degree of class consciousness considered peculiar in most American settings before 1929, but peculiarly suited in the 1930s to the articulation of mass insurgency; and as experienced trade unionists, they had a sense of the possible and a practical knowledge of organization missing in many American workers.

---

have talked with, German-born tradesmen seem more likely to have weathered the depression without serious difficulty.

   [39] Interview with Henry and Dorothy Kraus, 16 June 1986. Dorothy Kraus was chiefly responsible for organizing the auxiliary. Strike organizer John Anderson was supportive, but neither he nor the sit-downers at Midland Steel wanted women workers to participate in the plant occupation; they were relegated instead to the strike kitchen, the outside picket lines, and to community organizing. The auxiliary therefore marked a transition: the union recognized the familial dimension of working class solidarity, but still segregated women workers into the "domestic" roles deemed appropriate to their sex.

For these men, the absence of unions in American industry was not simply lamentable, but unnatural. Harry Southwell, the former member of the British Transport Workers Union who succeeded Walter Reuther as president of the UAW's West Side Local 174, later recalled his initial surprise when he arrived in Open-Shop Detroit:

> I immediately made inquiries as to the existence of a union, which an expert grinder ought to have been able to find without any difficulty, based upon my experience in England. I was rather amazed to find that while there was such an organization nationally, it had very few members and was very inactive . . . . This caused me quite a bit of concern because I had been led to believe through my upbringing that every group of workers aspired to some form of security through a union.[40]

Bill Stevenson, the Scottish toolmaker and 1939 strike leader at GM, also found the absence of a union "odd" when he arrived in Detroit, since in the Clydeside shipyards, where he apprenticed, workers could not get a job *unless* they were union members.[41] In a society wracked by industrial and social conflict, Stevenson's five-year apprenticeship, ending in 1921, went well beyond the technical and workplace concerns of the factory:

> The boys serving an apprenticeship in most of the shops on the Clydeside probably came under the supervision of a shop steward who at lunch time had classes on the industrial history of England, and its economic impact on society. So this was our training.[42]

It was a training that also included direct experience in mass mobilization against employers and, very often, the state. Matt Smith, the Lancashire toolmaker who organized and led the MESA—the first successful autoworkers' union in Detroit during the 1930s—travelled the entire gamut of political and trade union militancy before he left England. During World War I, he organized fellow apprentices into the Amalgamated Engineers, led several strikes, became a union officer, and

---

[40] Oral History Interview, Harry Southwell, 2, Reuther Archives, WSU.

[41] Typescript biography dated 20 August 1942, Vertical File, Bill Stevenson, Reuther Archives, WSU.

[42] Oral History Interview, Bill Stevenson, 4, Reuther Archives, WSU.

helped organize the national shop stewards movement that opposed the government's war aims; he paid for these actions in several jail terms for his refusal to serve in the British army and in a blacklisting that eventually drove him to Canada and Detroit. He was joined in this migration by others who had merged their trade unionism with opposition to the war, including the Scotsman Dave Miller, a former national leader of the textile workers union who spent three and a half years at hard labor in British prisons for his refusal to serve. Spurned in his native Dundee after the war, he too left for Detroit, where he later led the sit-down strike at Cadillac in 1937 and became the first president of UAW Local 22.[43]

Other British immigrant tradesmen followed a different path during World War I. Bill McKie, former member of the Sottish sheet-metal workers union and the Social Democratic Federation, served in the British Army during the war and was decorated for bravery. But McKie's left-wing and trade union experience in Britain also gave him a "sense of the possible" when it came to organizing the tool and die makers at the massive Ford Rouge complex in Dearborn, Michigan. When told on one occasion that the company's extreme repression made this task impossible, McKie made explicit reference to his British heritage. "I came from Britain," he replied. "There's a Labour Party there you know. That didn't rise by itself."[44]

Blacklisting, police repression, and prison were not "routine" matters for British and Irish trade unionists, but they were a fact of life these activists had been forced to confront long before they arrived in Detroit. This was especially true for those Irish immigrants who fought for the Republic during the rebellion and Civil War of 1916-1922. Pat Rice, a former IRA footsoldier, escaped the British Army by fleeing to the Canary Islands. By the 1930s, he had made his way to Detroit, becoming an operating engineer in the Ford Rouge power house and later winning election as president of Local 600's Maintenance and Construction unit. Hugh Thompson, another IRA veteran, came to Detroit in 1925, hired on at Murray Body

---

[43] Oral History Interview, Elizabeth McCracken, 3, 30-31, Reuther Archives, WSU; UAW Biography, undated, Vertical File, Dave Miller, Reuther Archives, WSU.

[44] Philip Bonosky, *Brother Bill McKie: Building the Union at Ford* (New York: International Publishers, 1953), 47 (quote), 19, 27, 125-128.

and helped organize the first federal AFL local at that plant in 1934. Pat Quinn, first elected president of Dodge Local 3—second only in size to Local 600—had joined the IRA at age seventeen and fought through the Civil War to the bitter end in 1922.[45]

The majority of Irish immigrants had not joined the IRA; some, like Michael Magee, had instead joined the British Army and fought in France during World War I. Even so, in the supercharged atmosphere of 1916-1926, Magee's membership in the Transport Workers Union and the British Labour Party brought him into direct confrontation with the state in 1926, when he played a leading role in the General Strike. For him, as for McKie, Quinn, Smith, Stevenson and other Anglo-Irish immigrants, the potential for a mass-based mobilization of workers was a practical experience, not a theoretical possibility. At the Ford Rouge plant, this experience quickly elevated Magee to positions of committeeman, executive board member, and vice president in Local 600.[46]

These foreign-born trade unionists left their imprint on Detroit's fledgling labor movement in many ways, both large and small. The MESA, one of the key nuclei around which the UAW in Detroit was later organized, took its structure from the British experience of the immigrant tradesmen who organized it. Elizabeth McCracken, office manager for that organization, later recalled Matt Smith's particular contribution:

> It was his influence, his British influence, that resulted in the Secretary's job being the most important job inside the M.E.S.A. . . . [H]e naturally chose to run for Secretary.[47]

Blaine Marrin, an American born toolmaker and member of Local 157, the key local in the 1939 GM tool and die strike, recalled that he "didn't know unionism from rheumitism" when he joined the UAW. Like many other American tradesmen, he was tutored by Local 157's three top officers: the Scotsman Bill Stevenson, the "Belfast" Irishman, Bob Crothers, and the Englishman, Bill Hulle. From parliamentary procedure to

---

[45] Babson, "Pointing the Way," 82-83.

[46] Campaign brochure, 1947 Local 600 election, and *Ford Facts* (2 October 1954) in Vertical File, Michael Magee, Reuther Archives, WSU.

[47] McCracken, Oral History Interview, 22-23.

strike mobilizations and strategy, these British tradesmen played a disproportionately large role in educating the first generation of American-born UAW activists.[48]

Marrin also recalled the prominent role in Local 157 of a German-born organizer Paul Dykes. Yet Dykes' German background was exceptional among early organizers, and the large number of German-born tool and die makers in the Fisher Body plant where Marrin worked were far slower than the British in rallying to the UAW. Culture and history account for much of this differential. Most obvious, German tool makers who had arrived in the United States in the 1920s did not speak fluent English and often found it difficult to conduct the most rudimentary exchanges with their fellow workers. Language set them apart, and their isolation was prolonged if they worked in one of the many German-owned job shops where even blueprints were in the mother tongue. Equally significant, the legacy of World War I and the anti-German hysteria was a recent and sobering memory for any German American who contemplated a high-profile role in the labor movement. Anti-Nazi feeling in America was also on the rise in the 1930s, especially among East European ethnics who viewed the resurgent "new" Germany with understandable alarm. Finally, immigrant Germans working in Detroit's toolrooms were not of one mind when it came to their relationship with non-German co-workers. Left-wing workers readily joined MESA and the UAW, and a few became prominent leaders. Pro-Nazi Germans spurned the UAW and a small number joined the German American Bund. The majority of immigrant Germans, on the other hand, assessed the risks and pursued a middle-of-the-road course that made them steady but relatively passive union supporters.[49]

In that regard, they were not unlike the majority of union members in the 1930s. Even in years of peak mobilization and mass action, workers never acted "as one"—perfectly unified and invariably militant. Most were pro-union and most favored action of some sort, but most were also aware of the labor movement's past failure to protect union activists from firing

---

[48] Interview with Blaine Marrin, 5 November 1985.
[49] Interview with Russ Leach, 22 October 1985; Interview with Blaine Marrin, 5 November 1985.

and blacklisting. Only a minority were willing to jump in front of their fellow workers and lead the way, and this initiating minority was disproportionately (though by no means exclusively) made up of tool and die makers and British immigrants. At Midland Steel, where, as previously noted, Scotsman John Anderson led the first sit-down strike in Detroit in November 1936, it was the toolroom workers—building on their MESA experience—who were first to organize 100 percent for the fledgling UAW. At Kelsey-Hayes Wheel, it was toolmaker Walter Reuther who led Detroit's second major sit-down, beginning in this case with a cadre of just ten activists who knew in advance of plans for the first "quickie" strike in this plant of 5,000 workers. The famous Flint sit-down that began a week after the victory at Kelsey Hayes initially closed only two plants in this GM stronghold, and in both cases only a committed minority of workers actually joined the occupations. After the Flint victory, in the far smaller but more numerous sit-downs in Detroit's tool and die job shops, the occupations usually began with a handful of organizers entering the plant and telling the workers to turn off their machines.[50]

None of these were "spontaneous" eruptions of militancy and all of them were initiated by an activist minority. Only when such initiating action proved successful was the more hesitant majority galvanized into action, and even then, an activist minority provided the leadership that held the strikes together. In March 1937, some 17,000 workers simultaneously occupied nine Detroit Chrysler factories in a carefully planned sit-down called by the UAW's national leadership. At Dodge Main, the biggest of these nine plants, Pat Quinn rose to leadership precisely because his previous IRA experience gave him the know-how and prestige which others recognized as the key to success. When one prominent local leader was revealed as a company spy, the strike committee called on "General Quinn" to establish the necessary security measures and discipline. "Our Chief of Police, Patrick Quinn, a former member of the Irish Republican Army, knows just how to deal with traitors," *Dodge Main News* announced to the sit-downers on the tenth

---

[50] *Midland Flash* (November 1936), 3; Victor Reuther, *The Brothers Reuther and the Story of the UAW* (Boston: Houghton Mifflin, 1976), 133-142; Marrin interview.

day of the occupation. "Get on your toes and let Pat do his stuff."[51]

Given the crucial role played by Quinn and other activists in initiating and sustaining the mass actions of 1933-1939, why has the myth of spontaneity been so durable? Part of the answer lies in the nature of these events, which quickly mobilized many thousands of workers in an exhilarating and partially successful campaign to reshape American society; in the afterglow of this heady upsurge, participants naturally celebrated the unity and vitality of the rank and file. But some participants also had reason to elevate the rank and file to a special prominence, ascribing to it an initiating role it did not always deserve, especially in the first sit-downs that paved the way for subsequent mobilizations. Union organizers in particular had reason to emphasize—and exaggerate—the unanimous and spontaneous support of the ranks for illegal actions which could easily land the real instigators in jail. Images of a unified and spontaneously militant membership also enhanced the union negotiator's bargaining position: "if you don't give us something to take back to the members, I can't prevent them from seizing another plant." All too often, historians, myself included, have uncritically taken this misleading testimony at face value.[52] It is, after all, an inspiring image.

Or is it? Consider how such tall tales of spontaneous militancy affect contemporary audiences, especially working class audiences. Do they see much "spontaneous" militancy around them today? Certainly not. Ironically, then, the myth of spontaneity, rather than inspiring action in the present, may only confirm the fatalistic conclusion that mass mobilizations

---

[51] Babson, *Working Detroit*, 80, 87-90; *Dodge Main News*, No. 9 (17 March 1937), 3.

[52] *The New York Times* on 10, 17, and 27 March 1937, quoted UAW leaders describing the Chrysler sit-down as spontaneous, and Jeremy Brecher, forgetting that these men faced conspiracy charges for their actual role in organizing and calling the sit-down, erroneously concludes in *Strike!*, 206, that such evidence confirms the spontaneous militancy of the rank-and-file worker. The actual sequence of events, in which plant committees carefully planned the simultaneous seizure of nine factories and union negotiators telephoned strike orders into the plants, was described in detail by the *Detroit News*, 9 March 1937.

are a thing of the past. In contrast, a focus on the actual dynamics of mass action, including the particular vectors of class, craft, and culture that motivate certain groups to initiate action, can open the way to both a better understanding of the past and a more productive appraisal of current possibilities.

Standard Cotton Products and the General Motors Sit-Down Strike: Some "Forgotten Men" Remembered

by
Kenneth B. West

Early in the morning of 30 December 1936, a group of automobile body workers sat down in Fisher Body plant No. 2 in Flint, Michigan, idling a thousand workers and stopping the daily production of 450 Chevrolet bodies. Later that day, workers similarly occupied the large Fisher Body plant No. 1, a facility which employed seven thousand men and women and produced fourteen hundred Buick bodies a day.[1]

These were some of the opening events in a drive launched by the newly-formed United Automobile Workers union to organize the General Motors Corporation and ultimately the entire auto industry. The ensuing strike was to last forty-four days. It would spread in and beyond Flint to involve 136,000 people in fifty GM plants across the nation, and it would culminate in an agreement with that massive company that would be characterized a day after the settlement as "the first major offensive won [by the Congress of Industrial Organizations, the CIO] in their program of unionizing the nation's basic industries."[2]

In the same story that reported the outbreak of strikes at Fisher Nos. 1 and 2, the local paper, *The Flint Journal*, also reported that during the afternoon of 30 December, workers in a small plant known as Standard Cotton Products Company also sat down following demands for a 20 percent wage increase, a minimum of fifty cents an hour, and an eight-hour day.[3]

Kenneth B. West is a professor of history at The University of Michigan-Flint.

[1] Sidney Fine, *Sit-Down: The General Motors Strike of 1936-1937* (Ann Arbor: The University of Michigan Press, 1969), 144, 304.

[2] *New York Times*, 12 February 1937, p. 1.

[3] *The Flint Journal*, 31 December 1936, p. 9.

In the fifteen years following the publication of Professor
Sidney Fine's book, *Sit-Down*, a great deal has been written on
the General Motors strike, but nothing has emerged to relate
the story of the strike at Standard Cotton Products. Fine
speaks of the 1930s when he refers to workers at Standard
Cotton as "the largely 'forgotten' workers," but they remain
forgotten in the pages of his book and have been neglected in
every account written since.[4]

This is understandable, however, because Standard Cotton
was a miniscule plant compared to the great auto complexes in
Flint. Employing perhaps 118 workers, they apparently played
no role in the strike strategy of the union, nor was their
participation significant in the general outcome of the strike.

Yet the story of the workers at Standard Cotton Products is
not without some interest. The vast majority of those in the
factory came from rural backgrounds with no prior union
experience. Miserable working conditions, however, made them
perceive the value of organization and moved them into the
UAW. They took advantage of a historic confrontation and sat
in their plant five days longer than the autoworkers. Their
determination won a contract which made a significant
difference in the quality of their lives. They deserve to be
remembered.

Their story cannot be based primarily on traditional written
sources. It can only be recovered through oral interviews with
those who were involved in the strike. I first became aware of
their story while working on a broader project on the
"insurgent rank and file" during the General Motors strike.[5] In

---

[4] Fine, *Sit-Down*, 317. For other extensive accounts of the strike see Sidney
Lens, *The Labor Wars from the Molly Maguires to the Sit-Down* (New York:
Doubleday, 1973); Irving Bernstein, *A History of the American Worker, 1933-
1941: Turbulent Years* (Boston: Houghton Mifflin, 1970), 519-551; Roger
Keeran, *The Communist Party and the Auto Workers Unions* (Bloomington:
Indiana University Press, 1980), 148-185. The most recent brief account is in
Ronald Edsforth, *Class Conflict and Cultural Consensus: The Making of a Mass
Consumer Society in Flint, Michigan* (New Brunswick and London: Rutgers
University Press, 1987), 157-176. For an interesting account written by a
participant in the strike see Henry Kraus, *The Many and the Few: A Chronicle
of the Dynamic Auto Workers*, 2d ed. with new preface and an introduction by
Neil O. Leighton, William J. Meyer, and Nan Pendrell of the Labor History
Project of The University of Michigan-Flint (Urbana and Chicago: University of
Illinois Press, 1985).

[5] The project involves Professors Neil Leighton and William Meyer of the

the files of the National Conciliation Service, I discovered a
letter written to President Franklin D. Roosevelt by employees
of Standard Cotton Products justifing their strike and
complaining of poor working conditions in the plant. It was
signed by forty-six men. A search for these men in the current
Flint phone directory uncovered seven still living in Flint and
these men pointed the way to a key figure, John Thrasher,
living in Fayetteville, Arkansas. All the men agreed to be
participants in oral interviews.[6]

Standard Cotton Products had been founded by two men,
Ellis Warren and Oscar Banfield, who had worked together
earlier making mattresses in Flint. Late in 1927 they
incorporated a firm known as Standard Auto Batts, and moved
into a building complex covering eight acres of land. The
property recently had belonged to Mason Motor Company, one
of the automotive enterprises of William Crapo Durant, the
founder of General Motors. The firm of Warren and Banfield
changed its name to Standard Cotton Products in 1933.[7]

The company manufactured auto batts—pressed cotton pads
sewn to burlap—which served as floor cushions and upholstery
material for the Chevrolet and Buick bodies made at Fisher
Body plants and for GM cars built in Lansing, Pontiac, and
Detroit, except for "a small part that was furnished by Allen
Industries of Detroit."[8] During the 1930s it discontinued the
manufacture of bedding and relied exclusively on the GM
market, though there is no evidence to suggest that the
company was financially controlled by General Motors.

Department of Political Science at The University of Michigan-Flint, and has
resulted in taped interviews with more than 150 veterans of the sit-down
strike. The tapes and some transcriptions are located in the office of the Labor
History Project at the university.

[6] The letter is to be found in the records of the National Conciliation
Service, File 182/2067, Box 418; National Records Center, Suitland, Maryland.
The following people were interviewed in the summer of 1980: Lloyd Gebo,
Earl Hubbard, James Humphrey, Walter Keech, Dolen and Maurice Scobey,
and Bruce Smelser. John Thrasher was visited in Fayetteville, Arkansas, in
February 1982.

[7] The story of Standard Cotton Products can be found in articles in *The
Flint Journal* for 22 December 1927; 23 August 1934; 22 May 1952; 9 January
1955. See clipping file on Standard Cotton Products in the library of *The Flint
Journal*.

[8] Letter from John Thrasher to the author, 29 June 1980.

The people interviewed agreed that perhaps 60 to 70 percent of the workers at Standard Cotton came from the South, more particularly from an area of about fifty miles between Paragould, Arkansas, and Malden, Missouri, around the Crowley Ridge of hills just east of the Ozark Plateau.[9] This was an area of rural towns and farms where the cutting of timber and the plowing of grasslands for cotton planting had led to severe soil erosion and forced lumbermen and small farmers to become day laborers, employed only for planting and picking cotton.[10]

In the later 1920s, as the auto plants were expanding, General Motors sent agents into these areas to recruit workers who were then sent by bus from places like Malden. They were used to hard work and the wages looked good compared to what they could make if they stayed in the South. Often they would be preceded or followed by fathers, brothers, cousins, or sisters who had married men who migrated north in hopes of a better life. Without skills, but used to long hours and poor pay, many of them would, by 1936, be listed in the *Flint Directory* as "laborer, Standard Cotton Products."[11]

Dolen Scobey came from a farm near Paragould in 1926 (along with two brothers-in-law) to work at Chevrolet for forty cents an hour. Later he went back to his father's farm for a few years, only to rediscover that it did not pay well. He returned to Flint in 1934 with his younger brother Maurice, and both were hired at Standard Cotton. A year later, a younger cousin, Bruce Smelser, came from Paragould. The thirty cents an hour

---

[9] Interview with John Thrasher, 27 February 1982. Lloyd Gebo and Earl Hubbard claimed the proportion was closer to 90 percent. See interviews with Lloyd Gebo, 25 April 1980, and Earl Hubbard, 24 April 1980. A sociologist, writing in 1983, claimed that Paragould was a focal point for migration to Flint. See Erdmann Duanes Beynon, "The Southern White Laborer Migrates to Michigan," *American Sociological Review* 3 (June 1983): 339.

[10] For discussion of this area see *Missouri: A Guide to the "Show Me" State*, compiled by the Workers of the Writers Program of the Works Progress Administration in the State of Missouri (1941; reprint, St. Clair Shores, Mich.: Scholarly Press, 1977), 327; and *Arkansas: A Guide to the State*, compiled by Workers of the State of Arkansas (1941; reprint, St. Clair Shores, Mich.: Scholarly Press, 1977), 292.

[11] Beynon, "Southern White Laborer," notes that 59.1 percent of 10,597 Southern whites in Flint in 1934 came up in the years 1925-1929. Annual directories are to be found in the Michigan Room of the Flint Public Library.

he received looked good to him; he had been cutting timber for forty cents a day to help support a family of eleven children.[12]

The Scobey brothers were hardly unique in their family connections at Standard Cotton. Of the signatures on the letter from Standard Cotton Product employees to President Roosevelt there were two Smelsers, two Thrashers, two Hubbards, and four Stegall brothers, in addition to many who were cousins.

James Humphrey and Earl Hubbard reflected the same migration patterns as the Scobey brothers. Humphrey, born in Malden, came to Flint with his father in 1927 after they had received word that General Motors was hiring. He quit school to join Standard Cotton that year. Then, in 1931, he was laid off and returned to Malden to farm for a few years. But "we couldn't make nothing. In fact we went into debt." He came back to Flint and Standard Cotton in 1935.[13] Earl Hubbard came to Flint from Malden with his father in 1928, when he was eleven. His father was employed as a sweeper in Fisher Body until he became ill. A lack of money and the need to support a large family caused Earl to drop out of high school and seek employment. For a few months he worked on a Works Progress Administration project at Bishop Airport, "moving dirt around," and then, in late 1935, having given up finding work at Chevrolet, Buick, or Fisher Body, he followed an older brother into Standard Cotton.[14]

Other former employees were from Michigan and their stories paralleled the ones cited earlier. Walter Keech and John Thrasher both lost their fathers when they were young. Both also had to quit school and take odd jobs to help the family survive. Keech was employed at Standard Cotton in 1930, but was periodically laid off. Thrasher was unemployed for a while, worked in the Civilian Conservation Corps for about a year, and got into the plant in 1935.[15]

Thrasher's brother-in-law, Lloyd Gebo, was born on a farm in Otisville. After the farm failed Gebo was employed as a laborer

---

[12] Interviews with Dolen Scobey, 28 August 1980, and Maurice Scobey, 24 April 1980.

[13] Interview with James Humphrey, 28 April 1980.

[14] Interview with Earl Hubbard.

[15] Interviews with Walter Keech, 4 June 1980, and with John Thrasher, 27 February 1982.

on farms in the area. He worked for about thirty dollars a month and all the food he could eat, but he often only received food because "deadbeat" farmers would not pay wages. He worked on Bishop Airport for the WPA and then moved into Standard Cotton just before the strike broke out.[16]

These men may not be typical of the workers who were in Standard Cotton Products at the time of the strike. They were certainly younger, had been in the plant for a shorter time, and were not leaders in the plant during the strike. Despite the fact that many of them had to work hard in their earlier lives, they had little experience with a disciplined factory environment.[17] They had few skills, could be easily replaced if they indicated dissatisfaction, and their experience left them with little understanding that a labor union might help them remedy some of their problems.

These workers had many grievances, however, and in retrospect John Thrasher claimed that "it wasn't too difficult to find reasons for organizing S.C.P.," though these reasons differed somewhat from the ones that would be most frequently suggested by workers in the auto plants in Flint.[18] Sidney Fine has concluded that in the auto plants ". . .it was the speed-up [of the assembly line] in the view of the principal participants that was the major cause for the GM sit-down strike." Similarly Henry Kraus stated that, "It was always the speed-up, the horrible speed-up. It was [this] that organized Flint, as it was the one element in the life of all workers that found a common basis of resentment."[19] The workers at Standard Cotton, however, did not complain of the speed-up; they did not work on an assembly line nor were they working on piecework pay, a practice which normally accompanied the speed-up.

Standard Cotton Products had the atmosphere of a southern cotton mill: low wages, long hours, and an unhealthy environment. A study of cotton mill workers noted that in 1936

---

[16] Interview with Lloyd Gebo.

[17] Dolen Scobey told me that when he was on a farm he worked hard, but "when you got caught up with the crops you was done for a few days." He and his brother Maurice both indicated they would have preferred that kind of work "if you could get a living out of farming." See interview with Dolen and Maurice Scobey.

[18] Letter of John Thrasher to author, 29 June 1980.

[19] Fine, *Sit-Down*, 55; Kraus, *Many and the Few*, 43-44.

hourly earnings in cotton manufacturing was 36.8 cents as compared to 56.4 cents in general manufacturing.[20] Workers at Standard Cotton claimed that their average was 43 cents an hour with some working for as little as 33 cents. They of course compared their pay with the pay of autoworkers in Flint, pay which was *higher* than the average in manufacturing, and pay which they almost invariably sought before accepting work in the cotton plant.[21]

These low wages might actually translate into a deceptively high weekly pay packet if one worked on the average day shift of fifty-nine hours a week or with the night crew of seventy or more hours a week. The night crew began work at 5 P.M. and worked until 7 A.M. the next morning with a half hour break for lunch. At rush times they might find a sign over the door as they left "if you want your job on Monday, be here Saturday and Sunday." Of course, there was no overtime pay.[22]

The work was subject to seasonal layoffs, however, since the auto plants often shut down for model changes and thus Standard Cotton had no work either. The depression years were notoriously subject to economic fluctuations, and many workers drifted in and out of the plant over the years. Thus, even in a reasonably good year, the workers would earn less than $1,000 a year.

All of this tedious, unrewarding labor was performed in rooms filled with thick cotton dust. Maurice Scobey said that the plant did not use real cotton but rather the sweepings off the floors of dye mills and threading mills, waste cotton full of dirt and even bits of metal. As this material was fed into shredders and then pressed into pads, clouds of dust arose which then settled over the floors, the machines, and the men. At night the light bulbs became reddish blurs, and one could only make out the silhouette of the man working next to him. The men wore masks but they were hot, uncomfortable, and did little to help breathing. Some men, who were interviewed for this paper believed that their present respiratory problems,

---

[20] Herbert J. Lahne, *The Cotton Mill Worker* (New York: Farrar & Rinehart, 1944), Appendix XI.

[21] Thrasher to author, 29 June 1980; *The Flint Journal*, 24 January 1937, p. 5.

[22] Interviews with Thrasher, Keech, and Smelser; *The Flint Journal*, 24 January 1937, p. 5.

such as emphysema, were brought on by their years at Standard Cotton.[23] Men worked in constant fear that a fire would break out from sparks caused by metal objects in the cotton being fed into the machines. Many fires did break out but there is no evidence that anyone was killed as a result.[24]

The machines themselves were not guarded, and according to Maurice Scobey, who lost part of one hand, "it was a bad place to get crippled up, you had better believe. The foremen were the first aid men if a man was hurt on the job."[25] Further hampering the workplace was the one toilet for more than 100 men, and lack of lockers, showers and a lunch room. Workers ate their lunches at their work stations or out in the hallway, though some did patronize a small grocery store about a block away.

Obviously these conditions would be considered intolerable by almost everyone and constituted sufficient grounds for protest organization and strike action. However, the men did not protest, according to John Thrasher, because if they did they would be told, "if you don't like it there's the door. We can hire someone else tomorrow."[26] In depression era Flint, these were not idle threats.

---

[23] Interview with M. Scobey. All of those interviewed commented on the choking cotton dust, but for especially pertinent comments on respiratory problems see the interviews of D. Scobey, Humphrey and Hubbard. In 1937, a Standard Cotton Products worker, Roy Kitley, claimed that cotton dust would eat "the inner lining out of a person in no time. A person can have a 100% health record before he hires in this factory [and] in two weeks after he obtains his job he is 50% under normal." See letter of Roy Kitley, 24 January 1937, in Henry Kraus Papers, Box 9, Walter Reuther Labor Archives, Wayne State University. This may be discounted as exaggerated special pleading, but Lahne, *Cotton Mill Worker*, 161, cites evidence that he claims "indicates clearly that cotton mill operatives had an abnormally high rate of mortality from respiratory diseases."

[24] Interviews with Hubbard, Humphrey, M. Scobey, Keech, and Gebo.

[25] Interviews with M. Scobey, Humphrey, and Thrasher. Hubbard said that after the union came in "we kept whittling away at 'em [on the safety problem] and they would put a . . . guard here and a guard there." Still Humphrey notes that well after the union came in Standard Cotton was still a dangerous place to work and that John Thrasher "nearly got killed in there" when he got caught in a press and it took about a half hour to extricate him. Thrasher showed me a mangled arm and said the accident crippled him for life and forced him to leave Standard Cotton. See Humphrey and Thrasher interviews, and Thrasher to author, 29 June 1980.

[26] Interview with Thrasher. While it is true that speed-up was probably the major grievance felt by autoworkers it should be noted that unhealthy and

Moreover, Thrasher had seen the futility of strike action in 1930 when some metal finishers and paint sprayers at Fisher Body No. 1 went out, and police on horseback ran down the pickets, broke up demonstrations, and chased strikers out of town. He, and others, were also reluctant to even talk about a union because you could never be sure that the man you talked to was not a "stoolie" for the company.[27]

Attitudes began to change in the summer and fall of 1936. A new United Automobile Workers union had been established and had joined the dynamic Congress of Industrial Organizations under the vigorous leadership of John L. Lewis. The organization promised a "new deal" for workers who had been regarded as "unorganizable" by the American Federation of Labor. Robert Travis and Roy Reuther came to Flint to contact workers and organize a big industry-wide local. Many auto workers responded when they knew a union was being formed that was not associated with the old AFL. Henry Kraus came to Flint to publish *The Flint Auto Worker*, a biweekly newspaper written to publicize the need for a union, and fifty thousand copies were delivered door-to-door.[28]

Small groups of three or four men from Standard Cotton went down to the UAW headquarters in the Pengelly Building in downtown Flint to hear these organizers talk about the advantages that a militant union could bring them, the power to transform their lives. Earl Hubbard went down to the Pengelly with five or six men in the summer of 1936 and joined right away. The Scobey brothers later went down with the Stegall brothers and joined the union. Each paid a one dollar membership fee and received a union button which they wore inside their shirts until numbers emboldened them to display them openly.[29]

Roy Reuther was especially popular with the Standard Cotton men, and all expressed their great affection for him.

---

dangerous working conditions were also prevelent among those who worked with presses, at buffing nickel, and in the paint department. See Kenneth West, " 'On the Line:' Rank and File Reminiscence of Working Conditions and the General Motors Sit-Down Strike of 1936-37," *Michigan Historical Review* 12 (Spring 1986): 71- 75.

[27] Ibid.

[28] For a recent account of the frustrations of autoworkers under the AFL and the new efforts of the CIO organizers see Edsforth, *Class Conflict*, 157-170

[29] Interviews with Hubbard, M. Scobey, and D. Scobey.

Bruce Smelser recalled that Roy "made the union sound so good you felt you couldn't lose." Robert Travis noted of his colleague that Roy took a special interest in Standard Cotton "and so we helped whenever we could. . . . "[30]

Some Standard Cotton workers were motivated by a sense of desperation, a feeling that they really had nothing to lose. Dolen Scobey equated his job to that of a coal miner, due to the dust in the plant. He believed that if he joined the union and got fired, he could simply return south and farm.[31]

On the day of the strike, Thrasher estimated that perhaps three-quarters of the workers at the plant were organized.[32] However, there was apparently no elaborate strike strategy to debate at Standard Cotton. As Robert Travis, leader of the UAW strike effort in Flint, noted, plans called for shutting down the plants that made bodies. This action naturally stopped delivery of cotton pads to General Motors and thus the men at Standard Cotton would be out of work regardless of any decision they might make.[33]

However, they did have a choice. They could have increased the ranks of the back-to-work Flint Alliance, and they could have written angry letters to *The Flint Journal* or the president as did many idled, non-union auto workers. Instead they decided to join the strike in hopes of improving their lot. James Humphrey felt he should take advantage of an opportunity. He was not in the union at the time of the strike but recalled, "We ain't gonna have any work anyhow so we might as well tie this place up and get some money out of it."[34]

The actual takeover of the plant took most of the men by surprise, though the men on the day shift heard rumors that Fisher Body plants were "going down" and many workers felt a strike was coming. Some strike leaders ordered the members of

---

[30] Interview with Smelser; interview with Robert Travis, 15 December 1978.

[31] Interview with D. Scobey.

[32] This may seem to be an unusually high estimate especially when compared with the 10 percent of the GM workforce estimated to have joined the UAW prior to the strike (Fine, *Sit-Down*, 118-119). However, it becomes more credible when one considers the terrible conditions under which the men worked and the smallness and homogeneity of the workforce.

[33] Interview with Travis, 15 December 1978.

[34] Interview with Humphrey. Yet Maurice Scobey indicated that when the strike finally came, "a few of the guys got scared and took off." Interview with M. Scobey.

the union to shut off the machines and occupy the plant while the day shift was on duty. The first news the night crew had of the strike, according to John Thrasher, a member of the night crew, was when they, "came to work and were asked to leave our lunches for the day crew so they wouldn't have to leave the plant to eat. . . . "[35] Unlike Humphrey, some non-union men did leave the plant when the machines stopped, but the majority of the day shift occupied the plant. The night shift served as outside pickets, made themselves available for emergencies, and later moved into the plant to take the place of some of the day men who had families.[36]

The men sitting in the plants were not compelled to stay in the plant. They could and did get passes to go home occasionally but were expected to return at a set time. Bruce Smelser remembers slipping out a couple of times to go to the movies, sneaking back in and never getting caught. Most of the men stayed in the plant, however, because no one had much money.[37]

Spending the strike time inside the plant was not bad according to one striker: "I enjoyed the strike. We had a lot of fun in there." There was no board to pay. The men had plenty of upholstery material to sleep on, and hot food was brought over by the union from some of the restaurants that catered to Fisher Body strikers. They kept themselves amused listening to the radio, reading, playing cards, putting on talent shows, and playing guitars and harmonicas they brought from home.[38]

Many songs came out of the sit-down strike and Standard Cotton had one of their own, a battle song set to the tune of "Four Thousand Years Ago." The following verses expressed the workers' sentiments:

> Oh, the cotton factory is a low-paid place,
> And the cotton it is staring you in the face.
> When you ask for more pay
> They would only turn away,
> For they think you can live and work this way.

---

[35] Interviews with Keech, Hubbard, and Thrasher
[36] Interview with Thrasher.
[37] Interviews with Smelser and Gebo.
[38] The interviews with M. Scobey, Smelser, and Hubbard were particularly informative on conditions inside Standard Cotton Products during the strike.

"Sleeping Quarters" Inside Standard Cotton Products, 17 February 1937

We worked fourteen hours a day.
But the Standard Cotton's going to change its way.
We've been working in the dust,
Now the machines are going to rust,
If the company don't settle up with us.[39]

The men had a roster of work assignments in the plant, but not all of the sit-downers were on that roster. A "kangaroo court" was set up to fine men who were late getting back to the plant after being out on a pass, and this court would impose penalties of washing dishes, sweeping, and cleaning up empty bottles after some had consumed a few beers.[40]

Time passed uneventfully except for one minor crisis. The plant was heated by hot water pipes encircling the inner walls and the water was heated by coal. When the coal ran out, the strikers called the management, which responded with what must have been relish, and told the men, "to go home and stay where it was warm." The response of the strikers was to open all the windows except for those in one room and inform the management that the pipes would freeze. The men, then, would keep themselves warm by burning costly burlap. As Thrasher recalls, "Coal got there in a hurry—several car loads of it."[41]

Morale was high during most of the strike and Standard Cotton did not feel forgotten at the time. Victor and Roy Reuther and other strike leaders visited them. The men on the outside mingled with strikers from other plants. A "hot line" was rigged up between the cotton plant and Fisher Body No. 1.[42]

Standard Cotton was ignored by those elements in the Flint community who sought to break the strike: the business community, the city government and police, and non-union workers who had been put out of work. The workers at Standard Cotton had no reason to complain of such inattention, nor did they feel they would be a likely target of attack. "We

---

[39] From "EB Songs," a compilation of songs put together by the Women's Emergency Brigade. The Labor History project is grateful to the late Sibyl Walker of the "EB" for making this available to us.

[40] Interviews with D. Scobey and Gebo.

[41] For accounts of this episode that vary somewhat in detail see interviews with Thrasher, Hubbard, M. Scobey, and Gebo, and letter from John Thrasher to author, 29 June 1980.

[42] Interviews with Smelser, Thrasher, M. Scobey, and Gebo.

knew if it happened it would happen to others in other bigger places first," said Dolen Scobey.[43]

They were very vulnerable however. They were few in number, the plant was easily accessible from the street with no fences around it, and they had few tools that they could improvise as weapons to defend themselves against an assault from police. Recognizing this, a couple of men suggested that the workers should bring their hunting rifles from home but this was quickly vetoed. The vast majority had no desire for a shoot-out.[44]

John Thrasher and others outside the plant were organized into a "flying squadron," ready to move to other plants at a moment's notice. He was called the night of 11 January, the night of the "Battle of the Running Bulls" when police tried unsuccessfully to force men out of Fisher Body No. 2. With hundreds of others from the city, Thrasher joined in the picket lines in front of the plant.[45]

It was this fracas that brought more than 3,000 National Guardsmen to Flint, where they stayed until the end of the autoworkers' strike. This caused a conflict of interest for John Thrasher because he had been a member of the guard for several years, and he was now called up for duty. He talked the situation over with Robert Travis and Roy Reuther. They decided that he could help the strikers by staying in the guard and talking to fellow guardsmen about working conditions that brought on the strike. When he was off duty, he would visit the Pengelly Building where he picked up copies of *The Flint Auto Worker*, the UAW strike paper, and distributed them to soldiers in the reading rooms and lounges of the armory. Once, late in the strike, he was caught inside Chevrolet No. 4 while in uniform, drinking coffee with some of the sit-downers, and for this he was severely reprimanded by the battalion commander. He derived real satisfaction when, as he remembered it, the last truckload of the guard infantry left Flint with some of the soldiers singing "Solidarity Forever."[46]

---

[43] Interview with D. Scobey.

[44] Interview with Gebo.

[45] Interview with Thrasher.

[46] Ibid., and letter from Thrasher to author, 29 June 1980. The story is partially corroborated by the interview with Gebo.

The Triumphant March at the End of the Strike, 17 February 1937

The guard left Flint after 11 February 1937, the date of the settlement with General Motors. The settlement did not come, however, until the UAW seized Chevrolet No. 4, the engine plant, and defied court injunctions to leave the properties. General Motors was anxious to get back into production since they had been losing markets to Chrysler and Ford, so an historic agreement was finally made recognizing the UAW as the bargaining agent for GM autoworkers, with exclusive rights to organize workers for a period of six months.

Workers at Standard Cotton Products were members of the large Flint local, but they were not covered by an agreement with General Motors, and some recalled a fear that the police might try to force them out of the plant. Rumors circulated that General Motors might buy their upholstery from a Detroit firm that was supplying Ford and Chrysler, and all the men would then lose their jobs.[47]

The men stayed in the plant for five more anxious days while thousands of autoworkers celebrated their triumph. They were cheered by visits from Norman Thomas, leader of the Socialist Party of America, who gave them inspiration and courage; from Rose Pesotta, veteran of many strikes; and from Roy Reuther, who did not desert them now that they needed him most. The men determined that after they had come so far they would not give up.[48] Finally, Standard Cotton Products, wanting to produce once again for the reopened GM plants, agreed to a two page contract. It was not as far reaching as the GM contract but it would be expanded and implemented over the next few years and would lead to some significant changes in the work lives of the employees.

A regular work week was now to consist of forty-five hours, composed of five eight-hour days and five hours on Saturday with time and a half for Sunday and holiday work. A minimum wage of fifty cents an hour was to be paid while generally wages increased 25 to 30 percent. In fact, Hubbard claimed that his wages as a machine operator doubled to about 65 cents an hour, though the wages did not keep up with GM workers. As Walter Keech put it, the smaller companies could not keep up with the larger companies.[49]

---

[47] Letter from Thrasher to author, 29 June 1980.

[48] Interviews with Thrasher, D. Scobey, M. Scobey, and Gebo.

[49] Interviews with Hubbard and Keech.

The work environment improved as well when "the company agrees to keep the toilets in sanitary condition and in perfect working order at all times." The company also agreed to install a hot water system for the washrooms, showers, lockers, and three drinking fountains. Most important, the company allowed its employees the right to belong to the UAW, to wear union buttons in the plant, and to appoint a bargaining committee to meet with management and to negotiate further improvements.[50]

Improvements did come as a result of continued negotiations. Guards were placed on dangerous machinery and something was done to alleviate, though not eliminate, the dust problem, when provision was made to inject a light oil spray onto the cotton before it was fed into the machines or pressed. On 15 October 1937 a new contract provided for a further adjustment of wages and hours, and *The Flint Journal* quoted Carl Thrasher, John's brother, as saying that the agreement was the "best yet signed in the cotton textile industry."[51]

The strike at Standard Cotton Products was not very dramatic, it was not filled with conflict, and its results were not very important for the general history of American labor. However, the workers who were involved deserve to be remembered. Without any experience in trade unionism but driven by a potent combination of misery and hope, they seized upon a critical moment in that history, converting it to their significant benefit. In cooperation with their fellow workers in the automobile plants, they did not "bring to birth a new world from the ashes of the old," but they did give an added meaning to the word "solidarity."

---

[50] A copy of the 17 February agreement is to be found in the Henry Kraus Papers, Box 10, Walter Reuther Labor Archives, Wayne State University. A discussion of the contract terms appeared in *The Flint Journal*, 17 February 1937. See clipping file on Standard Cotton Products in *The Flint Journal* library.

[51] All of the people interviewed commented on the benefits derived from the oil spray and the guards on the machinery. The contract of 15 October 1937 appears in *The Flint Journal* for that date.

Organized Racial Reform in Chicago During the Progressive Era: The Chicago NAACP, 1910-1920

by

Christopher Robert Reed

As early as its founding in 1909 the fledgling National Association for the Advancement of Colored People (the NAACP) formulated strategic plans for its future survival as a national organization. Part of this planning envisioned the creation of a network of strong local affiliates that would be formed as either vigilance committees or branches, with the former evolving into the latter after sufficient organizational growth had occurred. The broad responsibilities assumed by these affiliates included garnering local support for national civil rights issues, contributing substantially to the NAACP's finances, and providing a membership that was national in scope. With success at these tasks over the years, the branches earned the sobriquet of "lifeline of the Association."[1]

Chicago, as the Midwest Metropolis, was expected to produce a branch that contributed appreciably to the development of the NAACP. The city's antebellum generation had given it a reputation as a cauldron of abolitionism. At the dawn of the

---

Christopher Robert Reed is associate professor of history at Roosevelt University, Chicago, Illinois.

[1] Gunnar Myrdal, *An American Dilemma: The Negro Problem and Modern Democracy,* 2 vols. (New York: Harper & Brothers Publishers, 1944), 2:822. No written history of the Chicago branch of the NAACP exists but important scholarly references are found in Charles Flint Kellogg, *NAACP: A History of the National Association for the Advancement of Colored People, 1909-1920* (Baltimore: Johns Hopkins University Press, 1969), 124-5; Allen H. Spear, *Black Chicago: The Making of a Negro Ghetto, 1890-1920* (Chicago: The University of Chicago Press, 1967), 87-9; Arthur I. Waskow, *From Race Riot To Sit-In: 1919 and the 1960s* (1966; reprint, New York: Anchor Press, 1967), 46ff; Chicago Commission on Race Relations, *The Negro in Chicago* (Chicago: The University of Chicago Press, 1922), 148; and Thomas C. Holt, "The Lonely Warrior: Ida B. Wells-Barnett and the Struggle for Black Leadership," in *Black Leaders of the Twentieth Century,* eds., John Hope Franklin and August Meier (Urbana, Illinois: The University of Illinois Press, 1982), 54.

Michigan Historical Review   14 (Spring 1988)
Copyright © Central Michigan University 1988

twentieth century, Chicago still offered a setting in which
philanthropy, justice, law-abidance, and fair play were an
integral part of its heritage. The huge population of more than
one million persons contained Progressive whites who
demonstrated a willingness to devote both their influence and
wealth to the NAACP's cause. From their ranks the
abolitionist spirit was revived as neo-abolitionism. The burden
that the city's small black population of 30,000 shouldered in
resisting discrimination and recurring attempts at legal
segregation justified having a broad-based program aimed at
eliminating this civic affront. The consequent interaction
between progressive ideological acceptance and black
programmatic need produced the rationale for building an
organization. How this interest in racial reform was manifested
in the areas of ideology, organization, and program during the
Progressive era is a topic of historical importance and the
subject of this essay.

The Progressive coterie in Chicago that took an interest in
the NAACP was both interracial and interfaith in composition.
It included whites with direct ties to the abolitionist legacy of
the nineteenth century, as well as whites whose affinity to
egalitarianism derived from a modern intellectual or moral
base. The small number of blacks who favored egalitarianism
ranged from persons with a direct knowledge of slavery to
those who had a vicarious relationship as the offspring of either
free persons or slaves. Of the Chicago NAACP's nearly two
dozen egalitarian founders, only three had direct ties to
abolitionism. Jane Addams, the expected "mother" of the
Chicago NAACP movement,[2] was the daughter of an Illinois
abolitionist. Judge Edward Osgood Brown of the Illinois
Appellate Court, was a Massachusetts man by birth and son of
an abolitionist. Unitarian minister Reverend Jenkin Lloyd

---

[2] Bentley to Blascoer, 28 January 1911, Papers of the National Association
for the Advancement of Colored People, Library of Congress, Washington, D.C.,
Branch Files [hereafter NAACP MSS.]; Wells-Barnett to Spingarn, 21 April
1911, Wells-Barnett File, Joel E. Spingarn Papers, Moorland-Spingarn
Research Center, Howard University, Washington, D.C., [hereafter Spingarn
MSS.]; and Addams to Blaine, 11 October 1911, Jane Addams Papers (which
include portions of the Jenkin Lloyd Jones Papers, the Meadville Theological
School of Lombard, Illinois and portions of the W.E.B. Du Bois Papers, the
University of Massachusetts at Amherst), The University of Illinois at Chicago
[hereafter Addams MSS.]. Also see Kellogg, *NAACP,* 124, n. 30.

Jones had been a Michigan battlefield soldier whose abolitonist fervor was tested in combat. He steadfastly believed that "the war of freedom was not finished at Appomattox."[3]

Jane Addams' importance was such that the major precondition for the success of the Chicago branch was her active participation. Addams' interest in advancing the civil and social status of black Chicagoans antedated the formation of the black-led Niagara Movement in 1905 as well as the interracial NAACP in 1909. As early as 1903 Addams was actively involved with Reverend Jones and Ferdinand and Ida Barnett in challenging attempts to legally implement school segregation in the city's public schools.[4] She cooperated frequently with Atlanta University's W.E.B. Du Bois in efforts to build interracial understanding among black and white Chicagoans.[5] Although her vocation as well as her life's commitment was to Hull House, in the years preceeding the outbreak of World War I, Addams also developed strong ties to the international peace movement. Joining her in the peace movement as members of the Anti-Imperialist League were Judge Brown, Reverend Jones, and Reverend Celia Parker Woolley.

Three persons from the half-free, half-slave state of Kentucky also belonged to this group. Brown's fellow jurist, Robert McMurdy, was reared in Chicago and developed impeccable credentials as an egalitarian. His novel, *The Upas Tree* (1912), treated a black man as equal or more exemplary in character, intelligence, and dignity than the whites he encountered.[6] Willoughby Walling was the brother of William English Walling of New York who initiated the original call in 1909 for organizing a national egalitarian movement. Sophonisba Breckenridge, the third Kentuckian, was Dean of Women at the University of Chicago's School of Civics and Philanthropy

---

[3] *Chicago Defender,* 21 February 1914, p. 8 and 6 March 1915, p. 8.

[4] Addams to [Jenkin Lloyd] Jones, 20 October 1903, Addams MSS. Also, see Jones to Addams, 18 February 1906, Addams MSS. Further information is in Spear, *Black Chicago,* 45, 85.

[5] Addams to Du Bois, 25 January 1907 and Du Bois to [Addams], 2 June 1907, Addams MSS.

[6] Robert McMurdy, *The Upas Tree* (Chicago: F.J. Schulte & Company, 1912), 82, 83, 285, and 286. See also Bentley to Spingarn, 20 March 1915, Spingarn MSS. and *Chicago Defender,* 11 July 1914, p. 8.

as well as a cousin through marriage to Oswald Garrison Villard, the leader of the national body of the NAACP.

The other white founding members of the Chicago NAACP came from diverse backgrounds. They were held together by a commonality of belief that reason, justice, and morality were the proper regulators of thought and behavior. This reinforced their commitment to egalitarianism within the Progressive tradition. In addition, they were all from a social class stratum that was middle class or higher. The philanthropists, Mrs. Emmons Blaine and Julius Rosenwald, were much wealthier than their fellow egalitarians but N.W. Harris, a banker, Arthur T. Aldis, a real estate broker, and George Packard were also socially prominent.[7] Religious leaders such as Rabbi Emil Hirsch, the distinguished Hebrew scholar,[8] and Reverend Celia Parker Woolley, the founder of the racially integrated Frederick Douglass Centre located in the heart of the black south side community, endorsed egalitarianism through deeds at a time when it was not popular. The noted civil libertarian, Clarence Darrow, supported the branch as did Charles T. Hallinan, the editor of the *Chicago Evening Post,* one of the city's major newspapers. Active from the social work field were Addams, Breckenridge, and Woolley along with Charles T. Allinson, head of Booth house, which was located about a mile south of Addam's Hull House.

The leading black advocates of equality were Dr. Charles E. Bentley and Mrs. Ida B. Wells-Barnett. Both earned national reputations in the struggle on behalf of egalitarianism, were bitter personal foes of Booker T. Washington, and were given to obstinacy in their dealings with others. Bentley, a dentist, was recognized as the father of the oral hygiene movement which benefitted the nation's school children. Wells-Barnett distinguished herself as a journalist and played a singular role in advancing the anti-lynching crusade of the late nineteenth century. They differed significantly in their relations with whites. Bentley was at ease when working with the neo-abolitionists; Wells-Barnett was not.

---

[7] Albert Nelson Marquis, ed., *The Book of Chicagoans: A Biographical Dictionary of Leading Men and Women of the City of Chicago* (Chicago: A.N. Marquis & Company, 1917), 9, 266, and 520. The maiden name of Mrs. Blaine Emmons was Anita McCormick; she was one of the five McCormick children.

[8] Bessie Louise Pierce, *A History of Chicago: The Rise of a Modern City, 1871-1893,* 3 vols. (Chicago: The University of Chicago Press, 1957), 3:448, 449.

Courtesy of the Chicago Historical Society

Ida B. Wells-Barnett

Bentley's background offered a clear insight as to why he could interact on an amicable basis with whites. He was a child of antebellum Cincinnati, free persons of color, a person with a near-white complexion, and a professional who enjoyed a white downtown clientele as well as high status among whites both within and outside his professional circles. Bentley remained active within the branch's hierarchy until 1926, a period of service longer than any other egalitarian.

Wells-Barnett's background was totally different from that of Bentley's. She was the child of Mississippi slaves, an early feminist, a devoted wife and mother who temporarily forsook the racial struggle for motherhood and an egalitarian stalwart with an indomitable spirit regardless of the dangers. Hers was and never could be a world of compromise to injustice.[9] If Jane Addams was Saint Jane before WW I (before her peace efforts eroded her image) then Ida B. Wells-Barnett was Saint Joan d'Arc.

The two other blacks within the branch's hierarchy, Dr. George Cleveland Hall and Attorney S. Laing Williams, realized the need to fuse egalitarian ideology, which was more theoretical than practical, with conservative strategy. Hall was a surgeon at the all-black Provident Hospital, personal physician to Booker T. Washington when he visited Chicago, and promoter of the Chicago chapter of the National Negro Business League. Williams was an attorney who held his position of United States Assistant Attorney due to Washington's influence until the advent of the Wilson administration in 1913. While not a sycophant to Washington, Williams' respect for and loyalty to the Tuskegeean caused him to develop an animosity toward those individuals who opposed his patron along personal lines.[10] Williams was a complex

---

[9] Diary of Ida B. Wells, March 1886 and Wells-Barnett to Charles W. Chestnutt, 18 May 1915, Ida B. Wells Papers, Regenstein Library, University of Chicago. See also *Chicago Defender,* 8 March 1913, p. 1; 19 April 1913, p. 1; and 14 April 1931, p. 3. Full length treatments of Wells-Barnett include Alfreda M. Duster, ed., *Crusade for Justice: The Autobiography of Ida B. Wells* (Chicago: The University of Chicago Press, 1970); and Mildred Isabelle Thompson, "Ida B. Wells-Barnett: An Exploration of an American Black Woman, 1893-1930" (Ph.D. diss., George Washington University, 1979).

[10] S. Laing Williams to Emmett Scott, 25 October 1910, Booker T. Washington Papers, Library of Congress, Washington, D.C. For a fuller sketch of Williams' life, see Spear, *Black Chicago,* 66-69.

individual with equally diverse interests. He joined Dr. Bentley in the Equal Opportunity League in 1903 and by 1913 assumed the vice presidency of the Chicago NAACP.

In recent years, scholars have overlooked the importance of Jane Addams' role during the formative years of the branch's history while overemphasizing the influence of Julius Rosenwald. Along with Dr. Bentley and Ida B. Wells-Barnett, these four had the influence to shape, nurture, and maintain the NAACP movement in Chicago. Jane Addams used her influence to focus a substantial amount of public attention on the problem of inequality. In 1912, she hosted a three day national conference of people supportive of as well as curious about the NAACP's program and the ideology of egalitarianism that brought out the elite of Chicago's civic circles. Her friendship with Anita McCormick Blaine brought the national organization a benefactor during its most trying days financially. Addams was influential in the overlapping leadership circles of the city's social workers, social and civic elite, and publicists, thus sustaining the branch even when she was not personally active.

As to her character, Jane Addams once described herself before the war as having a "temperament and habit [that] had kept me rather in the middle of the road [on matters of contention]."[11] This tendency toward expediency led some contemporaries to lament their having followed her: "We had made the mistake in Chicago of considering Jane Addams as a moral leader and treated her as such and expected her to do in very difficult positions what a William Lloyd Garrison would do. . . . "[12] Because of her extensive pattern of activities, there was ample reason to understand why from time to time certain causes or issues received less attention. It was in this vein that her affiliation with the Chicago branch and the national office of the NAACP became a secondary consideration.[13]

Ida Wells-Barnett developed a deep disdain for blacks and whites who compromised their ideological fervor; and she was a

---

[11] Staughton Lynd, "Jane Addams and the Radical Impulse," *Commentary* 44 (July 1967): 57.

[12] As quoted in Allen F. Davis, *American Heroine: The Life and Legend of Jane Addams* (New York: Oxford University Press, 1973), 134.

[13] Telegram, Addams to Walter White, 27 June 1934, NAACP MSS.; Addams to Du Bois, 30 November 1914, Addams MSS.; and Kellogg, *NAACP,* 55.

critic of the branch until her death in 1930. Of the whites who looked to Addams for leadership, she wrote to Joel E. Spingarn, "I don't expect a great deal to result from their activity, for the very good reason that Miss Addams, who they desire to mother the movement, simply had not the time nor the strength even if she had the inclination to lead this new crusade." She continued stating that Addams' group merely wished to "bask in the light of her reflected glory and at the same time get credit for representing the race they ignore and withdraw themselves from in every occasion of real need . . . . I can not say that I look with equanimity upon their patronizing assumptions."[14]

According to Du Bois, hers was also a world of "persons who mean much within the veil [segregated America], but [were] less known without."[15] Wells-Barnett was active within the branch until after the 1912 conference, when she left the NAACP movement to pursue the cause of racial equality through other, all-black organizations. She devoted most of her time to her own Negro Fellowship League (founded in 1908) and as vice president in 1915 to the Chicago branch of the National Independent Rights League, a group headed nationally by Boston's militant, black egalitarian, William Monroe Trotter.

Julius Rosenwald's role and influence have been misunderstood and exaggerated in recent scholarship.[16] Rosenwald was unique in that he endorsed, without compromise, the conservative strategy along with an

---

[14] Wells-Barnett to Spingarn, 21 April 1911, Spingarn MSS., Wells-Barnett File.

[15] "[W.E.B.] Du Bois on the National [Negro] Conference, 1909," in Herbert Aptheker, ed., *A Documentary History of the Negro People in the United States*, 2 vols. (New York: The Citadel Press, 1961), 2:925.

[16] Two documents are used to support the contention that Rosenwald had an important role in and dominant influence over the Chicago branch. However, either separately or jointly, they simply do not substantively support this position. The documents are Bentley to Spingarn, 29 March 1915, Spingarn MSS., Bentley File and Memorandum, W.E.B. D[u Bois] to Spingarn, 2 April 1915, James Weldon Johnson Collection, Joel E. Spingarn Papers, Beinecke Rare Book and Manuscript Library, Yale University. The first document articulates Bentley's concern over one of Rosenwald's annual trips to Tuskegee Institute and its effect on the branch's leadership. In it, Bentley is unnecessarily alarmed and expresses his desire that his fear be shared with Du Bois. Four days later, presumably after Du Bois had read Bentley's letter, the

ideological commitment to greater opportunity, which was dependent on black self-preparation rather than on a theoretical equality. In 1914, he wrote to Villard that "there is no doubt in my mind that the work the [NAACP] is doing is extremely valuable, but other phases of service for individuals of that race are of greater personal interest to me."[17]

Julius Rosenwald's major commitment to the NAACP movement was financial. Significantly, his huge contributions were directed to the national office rather than to the Chicago branch. In his generosity he usually matched the contributions of other wealthy Chicago donors such as Mrs. Blaine, who yearly donated $1,000.00.[18] In 1914, he responded to a solitary appeal from the Chicago branch and contributed $325.27 to its operations. He was not asked to give again until 1920.[19] As a return for his support to the branch, Rosenwald wanted to approve the other members of the board of directors.[20] However, there is no evidence that he had influence of any magnitude over the board in regard to its composition. By 1917, his interest faded as William C. Graves, personal secretary to

Du Bois memorandum was written. The memorandum itself is a one sentence response to Bentley's worse apprehensions and warns Spingarn of the danger that both Rosenwald and Rev. Jenkin Lloyd Jones pose to egalitarianism and the branch. Strangely, DuBois's suspicions about Jones are inconsistent with his contributions to the branch and the NAACP movement. Kellogg cited these two documents in forming his view of the branch, *NAACP*, 124 and Holt, "Ida B. Wells-Barnett," 54, 61 was, no doubt, influenced by Kellogg. In addition, Holt was knowledgeable about Arvarh Strickland's description of Rosenwald and the Chicago Urban League in which Rosenwald is accurately pictured as having dominating influence over that organization. See *History of the Chicago Urban League* (Urbana, Ill.: The University of Illinois Press, 1966), 32ff. Ross also refers to Rosenwald's influence in Chicago but does not infer that it extended to include the leadership of the branch. See B. Joyce Ross, *J. E. Spingarn and the Rise of the NAACP, 1911-1939* (New York: Atheneum, 1972), 25-31.

[17] Rosenwald to Oswald Garrison Villard, 2 July 1914, Julius Rosenwald Papers, Regenstein Library, The University of Chicago, Chicago, Illinois [hereafter Rosenwald MSS.]. Also, "A Word From Mr. Rosenwald," *The Crisis* 4 (May 1912): 89; and Mae Nerney to Bentley, 11 May 1915, NAACP MSS., Adm. File: *Birth Of A Nation* Film.

[18] Addams to [Blaine], 7 August 1913 and Addams to Evans [for Blaine], 15 June 1914, Addams MSS.; also, Rosenwald to Villard, 18 August 1913 and 2 July 1914, Rosenwald MSS.

[19] W.C.G[raves] to Rosenwald, 26 January 1920, Rosenwald MSS.

[20] W.C.G[raves] to Rosenwald, 8 April 1914, Rosenwald MSS.

Rosenwald, stopped attending branch meetings due to their infrequency and unproductivity.

One noteworthy gesture Rosenwald made toward influencing the thinking of the branch's leadership came in 1915 when he led an entourage on his personal train to the Tuskegee Institute. Those accompanying him included some of the leading members of the hierarchy: Addams, Blaine, Brown, Jones, and McMurdy. The effect of the trip on those who went was reported by Dr. Bentley with guarded satisfaction. He observed that "nearly all—Judge Brown included—have been overwhelmed by what they saw without taking into account what it had cost . . . . I see the need for missionary work among the directory to the end that they see the whole picture. In this I have every hope, for at heart they want to know more of the question." Bentley's confidence in his fellow directors was buoyed also by the knowledge that a conservative speaker had visited the branch previous to the Tuskegee trip, and afterwards he could write that "the dreaded event has come and gone without injury to our policies and ideals."[21]

The ideology of the Chicago NAACP reflected its adherence to the ideology of the national body. Since this embodied a concept that the promise of a racially-egalitarian America should exist beyond theory and in actuality, the branch adopted a program that called upon it to work "for the advancement of colored people [at] efforts to lessen race discrimination and to secure full civil, political, and legal rights to colored citizens and others."[22] Ida B. Wells-Barnett, the well-known black egalitarian and feminist, saw in it a new hope for black advancement. She optimistically described it as producing "the new movement for our emancipation."[23]

Egalitarianism was an important, but minor, component of the progressive sentiment that pervaded the early twentieth century American mind. Even the NAACP admitted that "two lines of action [were] necessary for the emancipation of any

---

[21] Bentley to Spingarn, 29 March 1915, Spingarn MSS., Bentley File and *Chicago Defender,* 13 March 1915, pp. 1, 4.

[22] "Constitution of the Chicago Branch of the National Association for the Advancement of Colored People," 2 April 1913, p. 2, NAACP MSS., Branch Files.

[23] Ida B. Wells-Barnett to Joel E. Spingarn, 21 April 1911, Spingarn MSS., Wells-Barnett File.

individual and group or nation. First and foremost, the unfreed must himself strive, equip himself and advance. Secondly, the path before him must be cleared of dangerous obstacles."[24] The NAACP found its *raison d'etre* in the primacy of the second approach. The degree to which egalitarianism gained acceptance, however, depended on the place and the time it appeared. According to St. Clair Drake and Horace Cayton in *Black Metropolis,* egalitarianism did not garner substantial support in Chicago among blacks until the 1940s,[25] a period when even whites began to accept it more readily.[26]

The temper of the times in Chicago was such that egalitarianism had to coexist with the increasing tide toward involuntary segregation which accompanied Nordic racial supremacy, the constraints of WASP paternalism,[27] and the voluntary separation of black racial solidarity. In 1910, Dr. Charles E. Bentley, a leading branch spokesman, felt the need to constantly assess the organization's status in the city "in launching any new movement for a cause so unpopular as ours. But it must be done."[28] The next year Jane Addams wrote in

---

[24] "Sixth Annual report of the NAACP," *The Crisis* 12 (March 1916):246.

[25] St. Clair Drake and Horace R. Cayton, *Black Metropolis: A Study of Negro Life in a Northern City [Chicago]* (New York: Harcourt, Brace and Company, 1945), 763; notes from the lecture and question and answer session of St. Clair Drake's "How We Wrote Black Metropolis" presented on 6 November 1982 on the University of Chicago campus; and, John H. Bracey, "Black Nationalism Since Garvey," in *Key Issues In The Afro-American Experience,* eds., Nathan I. Higgins, Martin Kilson and Daniel M. Fox, 2 vols. (New York: Harcourt, Brace, Jovanovich, Inc., 1971), 2:266, 267.

[26] Peter J. Kellogg, "Civil Rights Consciousness in the 1940s," *The Historian* 42 (November 1979): 18-41.

[27] Typical of Chicago Progressives who were paternalistic in their views on blacks was H.C. Chatfield-Taylor, member of a prominent Chicago family of New England origins, member of the local sponsoring committee that welcomed the 1912 NAACP conference, and author of *Chicago* (Boston: Houghton Mifflin Company, 1917), 41, 50, 51, and 70. Also, see Addams, "Has The Emancipation Been Nullified By National Indifference," *Survey* 19 (February 1913): 566; Mary White Ovington, *The Walls Came Tumbling Down* (New York: Harcourt, Brace and Company, 1947), 106; *Chicago Tribune,* 11 June 1916, p. 8; and, Alfreda M. Duster, ed., *Crusade for Justice: The Autobiography of Ida B. Wells* (Chicago: The University of Chicago Press, 1970), 279-288. For a sampling of paternalism at the national level, see "The Bar Association and the Nation," *Outlook* (7 September 1912): 1.

[28] Charles E. Bentley to Frances Blascoer, 24 June 1910, NAACP MSS., Branch Files.

the same vein to Mrs. Emmons Blaine that "we have a little organization in Chicago, but we have yet done very little [here] .... You know, of course, how vexed the entire problem [of promoting racial egalitarianism] is and how necessary that some one should do some clear thinking and plan some decisive action in regard to it."[29]

By 1912, at the height of Progressivism, Oswald Garrison Villard, a leading spokesman of the NAACP, president of the *New York Evening Post,* and grandson of abolitionist William Lloyd Garrison, came to Chicago to address the fourth annual conference of the NAACP about its mission. At this pathbreaking, racially integrated convocation hosted by Jane Addams, Villard fervently announced that "Ours . . . is a battle for democracy, pure and undefiled. It is not for us to compromise, however much others feel the necessity for doing so."[30] Villard sought to rekindle the fervor of neo-abolitonism embodied in the national NAACP's Purpose which sought "to uplift the colored men and women . . . by securing to them the full enjoyment of their rights as citizens, justice in the courts, and equality of opportunity everywhere."[31]

This inclination toward ideological purity was understandable because of its indispensability to any organization's mission. In the case of the NAACP, its zealous abolitionist origins virtually dictated this mode of thought. The branch's core of leaders rarely deviated from this ideological stance, but when they did, it was due to a motivation to reconcile the pragmatism of American life and thought to the realities of black deprivation. Booker T. Washington's program of accommodation directly attacked the problem of economic deprivation so it was not seen as a threat but rather as a complementary strategy by some branch leaders.

At a branch meeting in 1914, Professor Joel E. Spingarn of New York even explained to Chicagoans that "idealism it is the function of the [NAACP] to kindle. Mr. Washington is doing a

---

[29] Jane Addams to [Anita McCormick] Blaine, 3 February 1911, Addams MSS.

[30] Oswald Garrison Villard, "The Objects of the National Association for the Advancement of Colored People," *The Crisis* 4 (May 1912): 82.

[31] "First Annual Report of the National Association for the Advancement of Colored People," 1 January 1911, Anita McCormick Collection, State Historical Society of Wisconsin, Madison, Wisconsin [hereafter Blaine MSS.].

needed work in making a strong and prosperous people from which the Association may recruit strength. But the two sides of the general movement must thus supplement each other, for together they represent the balance of utilitarianism and idealism which is the characteristic gait of American progress."[32] Only Wells-Barnett, Bentley, and McMurdy were so ideologically rigid as to reject Washington's program totally. To these stalwarts the conservative strategy was unacceptable because it placed an inordinate burden upon blacks to prove their moral and material worthiness for eventual, rather than immediate, citizenship rights.

Scholars have interpreted disagreements over which strategy the blacks should endorse for their advancement as schismatic, with a Washington camp in opposition to a Du Bois following. However, the discord was never that divisive. Contemporary editorials in the *Chicago Defender* and *Chicago Broad-Ax* captured the essence of the black community's feelings when they explained that Washington's strategy "represented a line of thought that was essential to the masses living under the conditions from which he arose." When radical and conservative strategies were evaluated the newspapers commented that, "both were necessary to complete the armament of this oppressed race . . . why the hysteria from the advocates of either plan for race advancement; surely both have our interests at heart, and both being earnest and zealous why let the zeal become embittered . . . . "[33]

Attorney Earl B. Dickerson, who devoted more than two-thirds of his ninety-five years in the service of egalitarianism under the banners of both the Chicago branch and the national office of the NAACP, reflected in 1984 that there was never

---

[32] "Opinion," *The Crisis* 7 (March 1914): 227. The view of Spingarn as the uncompromising champion of egalitarianism and carrier of the torch of "new abolitionism" is best seen in Ross, *Spingarn*, 21-48.

[33] *Chicago Defender*, 10 January 1914, p. 4 and *Chicago Broad-Ax*, 7 September 1912, p. 1. See Spear, *Black Chicago*, 84ff. and Strickland, *Chicago Urban League*, 34ff. for views that support the contention that a split among the black elite was of great importance in black Chicago. For a view that holds that the split was of major importance on a national scale, see the definitive work on the subject by August Meier, *Negro Thought In America, 1880-1915: Racial Ideologies in the Age Of Booker T. Washington* (Ann Arbor: The University of Michigan Press, 1963), especially Chapter 10, "Radicals and Conservatives."

any sense of urgency among Chicagoans to choose between the strategies.[34] This interpretation was further supported by St. Clair Drake two decades after the Progressive period.[35] The blacks of Chicago had a tradition of viewing economics coupled with racial solidarity and self-help as components of a strategy of egalitarian advancement.[36] This situation existed before Booker T. Washington made his historic Atlanta Address (1895) and established his National Negro Business League (1900). From the pages of the *Chicago Conservator* and Isaac C. Harris' *Colored Men's Professional and Business Directory* in the late nineteenth century to those in the *Chicago Defender* and *Broad-Ax* during the Progressive period, continuous pleas were made for support of this strategy to prove to blacks and whites alike that blacks as a group were worthy first, of respect for assuming responsibility for their destiny and second, of recognition of their birthright to citizenship.[37]

Shortly after the turn of the century, a small group of black entrepreneurs emerged and belatedly spread the "Gospel of Wealth," both in word and deed. Significantly, these activities took place independent of the Tuskegee program with which they agreed. The spirit in the commercial sector was matched by a fervor among the masses that manifested itself in a desire for freedom from white interference in black affairs rather than an interest in racial equality. Not unexpectedly, the black rank and file, which was supposed to fill the branch's membership list remained aloof, primarily because they accepted voluntary

---

[34] Interview with Mr. Earl B. Dickerson in his corporate office on 21 March 1984, in Chicago. Dickerson knew both Washington and Du Bois, having taught at Tuskegee in 1914 and having interacted with Du Bois as a fellow NAACP supporter. Dickerson led the legal redress committee of the Chicago branch in the 1930s, was part of the legal team that prepared *Hansberry v. Lee* (1940), and served at the national level on the board of directors.

[35] St. Clair Drake, *Churches And Voluntary Associations In The Chicago Negro Community* (Chicago: Works Progress Administration, 1940), 125.

[36] Spear, *Black Chicago*, 60.

[37] For some examples see *Chicago Conservator,* 23 December 1882, p. 4; I[saac] C. Harris, comp., *The Colored Men's Professional And Business Directory of Chicago* (Chicago: I.C. Harris, Publisher, 1885 and 1886), preface page; D.A. Bethea, comp., *The Colored People's Blue Book* (Chicago: Celerity Press, 1906), 7, 8; and, the description of Booker T. Washington's appearance in Chicago in 1912, *Chicago Broad-Ax,* 24 August 1912, p. 2. It was common for both the *Chicago Defender* and *Chicago Broad-Ax* to lionize such rising entrpreneurs as Jesse Binga with regularity.

separation as a way of life. This fatalism stemmed from their experiences in both the South and Chicago. Whether in the work place, where they were excluded from industry and relegated to service occupations until World War I, or in their search for housing, where they found themselves restricted to undesirable enclaves throughout the city, blacks were continually forced to accept their powerlessness. This pattern was repeated in politics and education, where the lack of representation and the recurring threat of segregation, respectively, were major problems. Ideology thus provided as well as undermined the rationale for building an egalitarian organization.

The Chicago NAACP began its organizational existence in 1910 as a vigilance committee. It was composed of some of the city's leading publicists, among whose ranks were Addams, Hallinan, Wells-Barnett, Jones, and McMurdy. The structural evolution from a vigilance committee began with the formation of a branch in 1912 and the issuance of a charter from New York in April 1913.[38] During the period from formation to charter, the egalitarians neither developed a program of action nor engaged in any protest activities. Their energies were directed inwardly to basic organizational matters. They wrangled constantly over the structure, method of operation, and constitution of the organization.

Willoughby Walling espoused his support for an organization that would follow closely the "ideas of my brother."[39] Adoption of this approach meant that activism would have preceded the establishment of a structure.[40] The Walling position differed considerably from that of Dr. Bentley, who had been the architect of the twentieth century's first black advancement movement, the Niagara Movement.[41] Bentley wanted an organization that first concentrated on raising funds, disseminating information, building membership, and garnering prestige among all Chicagoans; later the

---

[38] Note 3 and "Notes on [the] Chicago Branch," 15 February 1936, NAACP MSS., Branch Files.

[39] Bentley to Blascoer, 28 January 1911, NAACP MSS., Branch Files.

[40] Kellogg, NAACP, 43, 44.

[41] Also see W.E.B. Du Bois, "The Voice of the Negro," September 1905, p. 619 cited in Philip S. Foner, ed., W.E.B. Du Bois Speaks: Speeches And Addresses, 1890-1910 (New York: Pathfinder Press, 1970), 144.

organization could engage in activities that promoted equality. Bentley's approach, which appealed to the influential, if not the circumspect among the leadership, was accepted.

Once the branch began its operations, several weaknesses were evident. The reliance on a volunteer group to run the branch in the style of the national office was the most obvious.[42] This pattern was attempted despite the professional commitments of Brown and McMurdy, who were sitting judges; Hallinan, who ran a newspaper; Addams, Woolley, Allinson, and Wells-Barnett, who administered to the affairs of settlement houses; Williams, who was a struggling attorney; Jenkins, who at age seventy in 1913 was still called to preach; and, Hall and Bentley, who had to tend to their medical practices. Most significant, though, was the absence of a paid executive secretary and a permanent office from which daily activities could be conducted. This feature hampered both the growth of the organization and the implementation of the NAACP's program.

By 1917, the branch was languishing to such an extent that Judge Brown, the president from 1913 to 1922, felt inclined to write to Dr. Arthur B. Spingarn in New York that "we need inspiration and encouragement for our work such as [only] you can give us."[43] The next year Bentley corrected part of the branch's structural problems with a "reformed plan."[44] Bentley's plan laid the groundwork for a permanent secretary and office. The office was opened in 1919 under the direction of a young Louisianan, A.C. MacNeal. MacNeal was a Yale graduate and destined to be the branch's most active president before WW II. Despite this short "awakening," the national office regarded the branch as being "dead" by the summer of 1920, and subsequent consideration was then given to the possible removal of the branch's charter.[45]

---

[42] Ross, *Spingarn,* 56, 57, 68, 69; Ovington, *Walls,* 109-111; and, Kellogg, *NAACP,* 42, 61.

[43] Edward Osgood Brown to Arthur B. Spingarn, 10 January 1917, Spingarn MSS., Brown File.

[44] Bentley to James W. Johnson, 18 March 1918, NAACP MSS., Branch Files.

[45] W.C. G[raves] to Rosenwald, 26 January 1920, Rosenwald MSS. and Robert W. Bagnall to Johnson, [no date], but in with material marked 1910-1921, NAACP MSS., Branch Files.

Courtesy of the Chicago Historical Society

Jane Addams, ca. 1915

The qualitative leadership to direct the branch that should
have emerged from the ranks of the city's Progressives did not
because of the constant departure or lack of involvement of key
personnel. The prescribed rotation of officers unfortunately
failed to provide replacements. Both Addams and Wells-Barnett
were inactive by 1913, just a year after formal organization.
Subsequently, Woolley resigned. When the two-year terms of
Blaine and Hallinan on the Executive Committee (the body
that superseded the Board of Directors as the governing unit of
the branch) expired, they severed their ties to the organization
altogether.[46] The drain on leadership continued with the
departure of Dr. Hall and Julius Rosenwald's representative on
the board, William C. Graves. Most often, even in the case of
the latter two members, theirs was not an alienation as to the
direction of the program as much as a gnawing displeasure
with organizational inactivity. Finally, S. Laing Williams, the
branch's only active attorney who challenged discrimination
through the courts, left midway through the decade to pursue
his private practice.

The operations of the branch were left in the hands of a
select few: Brown, Bentley, McMurdy, and Jones. All were able
and enlightened men, but aging. The age factor was to have an
effect on the industriousness, or lack of it, that was manifested
in running the organization and program. While New Yorkers
in the national office averaged thirty-five years of age in 1909,
the Chicagoans averaged fifty-three.[47] Significantly, because of
the limited support provided the branch by Chicagoans,
whatever these stalwarts did became the sum of the branch's
activities and accomplishments.

The structure of the organization called for working
committees to carry out the branch's program. Committees on
membership, legislation, and legal grievances were established
in 1913. A fourth committee on education was formed in 1914
to fight the growing public sentiment favoring segregation in
the public schools. Before Hallinan left in 1915, he handled the
branch's publicity as chairman of the press service. In his able
hands, news of the Chicago branch appeared in *The Crisis,*

---

[46] *Chicago Defender,* 30 April 1915, p. 5.

[47] Kellogg, *NAACP,* 90, 91. Chicago members and their birthdates: Jones,
1843; Brown, 1847; Bentley, 1859; Addams and McMurdy, 1860; and Wells-
Barnett, 1862.

Chicago Defender, Chicago Broad-Ax, Chicago Evening Post, and *Chicago Tribune.*

The work of the membership committee was not performed so ably. This committee was composed of persons of limited influence and stature in the city such as S. Laing Williams, George R. Arthur of the black YMCA, and Thomas Allinson of Henry Booth Settlement House. Their failure was evidenced by the branch's small membership which consisted of only 275 people in 1916.[48] The number of sympathizers was larger, however, as indicated by the number of subscriptions to *The Crisis* in 1914 which showed Illinois as having the largest readership nationally.[49]

It did not appear that Bentley's plan to absorb the men of the defunct Niagara Movement into the branch was successful, indicating that black middle-class support was tenuous. The mass enrollment of thirty-eight chair car porters from the Northwestern Railroad in 1914 augmented the small membership. They evidently had responded to the branch's efforts to save their jobs from a racist attempt at occupational elimination. This significantly demonstrated that the working class could be attracted to the organization's cause if it aided theirs. Perhaps Bentley had this in mind when he formulated his reorganization of 1918 which ambitiously hoped to attract as many as 2,000 members. Bentley's projection proved illusory though as the branch ended the decade without any appreciable increase in its ranks.

The finances of the branch, which were to have come from the membership as well as from wealthy white supporters such as Blaine and Rosenwald, also proved to be limited. There was a shared belief among a large number of blacks that the responsibility of financing an egalitarian organization rested in the hands of white philanthropists.[50] During the summer of 1914, a street carnival was held to counter this sentiment and it helped fill the treasury slightly. The carnival also heralded the active participation of postal workers such as Archie Weaver, along with that of A.C. MacNeal, proving by the 1930s

---

[48] *The Crisis* 12 (March 1916): 257.

[49] Ibid., 10 (June 1915): 97. By 1917, Illinois was in a distant third place according to figures in *The Crisis* 15 (December 1917): 93.

[50] Bagnall to Johnson, 2 January 1920, NAACP MSS., Spec. Corres.: Bagnall.

that the trying days of Progressivism were not totally unproductive.

While the branch lacked support and recognition from the majority of the city's citizenry, the established institutions of the black community did not. Blacks consistently sought out Robert S. Abbott of the *Chicago Defender,* Wells-Barnett at her Negro Fellowship League, and Frank Hamilton of the Appomattox Club for assistance and leadership in obtaining their rights.[51] While a few black Progressives were attracted to the Chicago NAACP, other well-trained and educated blacks with ethnocentric leanings gravitated toward the Appomattox Club. This organization had been established by Edward Wright, formerly of New York City, in 1900 as a meeting place for the newly rising black professional leadership. Rising racial consciousness among all strata of blacks led to a preference for this type of organization. Yet, the presence of these all-black groups neither implied competition with nor antagonism toward the Chicago NAACP. To the contrary, what emerged from the ranks of the black elite was a spirit of cooperation with white egalitarians which showed that the seeds of equality were firmly implanted in Chicago.[52]

External pressures affected the branch as much as internal ones. The war years brought ideological enervation to Progressivism generally and to neo-abolitionism specifically. To many Progressives the struggle against inequality at home seemed of less importance than first, eliminating totalitarianism in order "to make the world safe for democracy;" second, ending the brutality of war itself, as advocated by peace advocates Addams, Blaine, Jones, and Hallinan; and third, assisting the southern migrant in adjusting to urban life.

---

[51] See examples in the *Chicago Defender,* 11 July 1912, p. 1; 12 October 1912, p. 1; 19 April 1913, p. 1; 11 October 1913, p. 1; 17 January 1914, p. 1; 17 April 1915, p. 1; 15 January 1916, p. 10; 17 June 1916, p. 6; 27 January 1917, p. 1; and, 3 November 1917, p. 7. Also see the *Chicago Broad-Ax,* 26 April 1913, p. 1.

[52] See examples in the *Chicago Defender,* 8 March 1913, p. 2; 12 April 1913, p. 1; 2 August 1913, p. 7; 18 October 1913, p. 4; 4 April 1914, p. 1; 17 April 1915, p. 1; and 6 November 1915, p. 8. Also, see the *Chicago Tribune,* 14 June 1916, p. 8. The emergence of a group of blacks who were receptive to egalitarianism belonged to the "New Negro" phenomenon which was covered by Meier, *Negro Thought,* 276, 277.

With America's 1917 entry into the war, the national NAACP succumbed to the general pro-war argument as well as to the black conservative legacy of Booker T. Washington. Du Bois and Joel Spingarn (who subsequently fought in the war) reversed themselves and accepted the government's proposition that segregated training camps for black army officers was not a step backward in race relations. They argued that there would be no black officer corps to lead the black troops without the special camps, so these leaders allowed ethical relativism to dominate their reasoning. In response to critics, Du Bois wrote editorially in *The Crisis* that "If we organize separately for anything—Jim Crow scream the Disconsolate; if we organize with white people—Traitors!... yell the Suspicious; If unable to get a whole loaf we seize half to ward off starvation—Compromise! yell all the Scared. If we let half the loaf go and starve—why don't you do something? Yell the same critics...."[53]

This argument failed to persuade black Chicagoans. Drs. Bentley and Hall rejected the concept of segregated camps at a May 1917 meeting in Chicago. Robert Abbott of the *Chicago Defender* commented that "something is wrong when loyal, patriotic citizens, ready and able to fight, are compelled to petition their government for an unprescribed approval to fight for it."[54] According to Bentley's biographer, when Bentley was confronted with the probability of having to examine white and black soldiers in separate dental facilities, he became indignant.[55]

The war-induced migration produced an increase in Chicago's black population between 1910 and 1920 of 148.5 percent as the number of blacks in the city rose from 44,103 to 109,458. It affected the Chicago NAACP by relegating the branch even more firmly into a secondary role in the lives of black and white Chicagoans as racial tensions were exacerbated on the job site, in recreation, and in housing. By 1916-1917 egalitarian Progressives developed a strong interest in the

---

[53] *The Crisis* 14 (June 1917): 61. Also, Ross, *Spingarn*, Ch. 3 and Kellogg, *NAACP*, Ch. 11.

[54] *Chicago Defender*, 7 April 1917, p. 12; 28 April 1917, p. 1; and 26 May 1917, p. 1.

[55] Clifton O. Dummett, *Charles Edwin Bentley: A Model For All Times* (St. Paul, Minn.: North Central Publishing Company, 1982), 184, 185.

Urban League idea which emphasized economic and social adjustment to urban life rather than a struggle for equality. With so many newcomers in the city, even Judge Brown was calling the adjustment effort "of the highest importance to the Negro."[56] Jane Addams wrote to Anita McCormick Blaine eliciting her support by observing "the condition of the newly migrated Negro is an especially helpless one."[57] The idea of a league soon received Rosenwald's support and Graves was urging persons with whom he corresponded in Rosenwald's behalf not "to confuse the Chicago Urban League with the NAACP [which is burdened by] chronic inactivity [when assistance is needed by blacks immediately]."[58]

The *Defender* clamored for an Urban League affiliate to be established in Chicago as public concern and support grew. So, by 1917, many of the founding members of the Chicago NAACP were found among the active sponsors of the newly organized Chicago Urban League: Addams, Brown, Hall, Woolley, Breckenridge, Rosenwald, and Blaine became members of the board of directors.

The extent of change was further illustrated by the ironies of the situation. The first president of the Chicago Urban League, Professor Robert E. Park of the University of Chicago's Department of Sociology, had been a secretary to the late Booker T. Washington. And in 1918, 'Celia Parker Woolley offered the league the facilities of the Frederick Douglass Centre as its headquarters. A decade and a half earlier, Woolley had established the center as an example of how beneficial and easily facilitated egalitarian contact could be between the races. It was at the center that the Bentleys, Williamses, and Barnetts had had their most extensive contact with egalitarian white Progressives.[59]

Both the internal and external difficulties that hampered the Chicago NAACP in its organization also affected the quality of its program. Inactivity bred greater inactivity instead of an activism that was consistent with the expectations of

---

    [56] Brown to Charles G. Dawes, 14 December 1916, Rosenwald MSS.
    [57] Addams to Blaine, 18 August 1917, Rosenwald MSS.
    [58] W.C. G[raves] to Rosenwald, 23 November 1917, Rosenwald MSS.
    [59] Duster, *Crusade for Justice,* 279-288. Also, "Celia Parker Woolley's Work," *Chicago Defender,* 27 March 1915, p. 8 and *Douglass Centre Fall Calendar,* 1907, n. p., Blaine MSS.

egalitarian strategy. The branch's program had a life span that covered clusters of months instead of years. A contemporary assessment of the branch by the Chicago Commission of Race Relations indicated that significant activities took place only after the riot of 1919. At that juncture in its history the branch led the challenge against maladministration of justice of black riot defendants.[60] Allen Spear's *Black Chicago*, published in 1967, focused on the branch's heightened activities around 1913.[61] Most important, guidelines established for all branches by the national NAACP office in 1913 made an updated evaluation possible for this essay.[62]

Branches were expected to perform twelve principle functions to be considered effective components of the NAACP lifeline, especially in regard to mounting legal redress to cases of discrimination and segregation. Of the twelve guidelines, the Chicago NAACP adhered to only half. In 1913, legislative activities occurred as the branch cooperated with the Appomattox Club in the state capital to stop discriminatory laws from being passed that affected jobs of black trainmen, interracial marriage, and the enactment of other Jim Crow prohibitions.[63] The branch was also involved in two discrimination cases. The first occurred in 1914 when S. Laing Williams brought suit against a downtown hotel that refused accommodations to an Ohio State University student in the city for sports competition. The second occurred in 1917 when Bentley, Brown, and McMurdy acted on behalf of a black physician who was prevented from serving in his position at the Chicago Municipal Tuberculosis Sanitarium.[64] The branch did prove somewhat effective, but only over a short period, in disseminating propaganda and information and in holding amicable interracial meetings.

Unfortunately, the branch neither acted in accordance with the guidelines nor with the black community's wishes in encouraging greater job opportunities, fuller participation in

---

[60] Chicago Commission on Race Relations, *The Negro In Chicago*, 148.

[61] Spear, *Black Chicago*, 88.

[62] *The Crisis* 6 (May 1913): 27, 28.

[63] *Chicago Defender*, 21 June 1913, p. 8; and 29 August 1914, p. 7. Also, *Chicago Broad-Ax*, 26 April 1913, p. 1.

[64] *Chicago Defender*, 21 June 1913, p. 8; and 29 August 1914, p. 7. Also, *Chicago Broad-Ax*, 26 April 1913, p. 1.

the academic aspects of education, or heightened involvement in political matters. So, throughout the decade, groups other than the Chicago NAACP were just as, if not more, active on behalf of civil rights advocacy. During March 1914, when Williams was seeking redress for the Ohio State University student, the *Defender's* staff was investigating the new use of films as a propaganda device to promote Nordic supremacy and black inferiority. This antedated the branch's efforts against the infamous *Birth Of A Nation* by a full year.[65] Even in 1915, while the leadership of the branch was approaching newly elected mayor William "Big Bill" Thompson about the film, Illinois state Representative Robert Jackson was introducing a bill before the General Assembly to prevent the showing of inflammatory racial films.[66] While the branch's efforts against the film were faltering with *Birth Of A Nation* being shown regularly, Jackson persisted until by 1917, his bill was enacted—over formidable opposition—to prevent the showing of all films of this type.[67] Jackson's activities marked the introduction of organized black Republican protection of the civil rights of blacks. The election of Oscar De Priest to the Chicago City Council in 1915 meant that discrimination and segregation would now be fought by blacks on two levels of government.[68] Lastly, when the East St. Louis, Illinois, riot occurred in 1917, the branch responded by sending $200,000 in aid while the *Defender* sent Ida B. Wells-Barnett to investigate and lend assistance on the scene.[69]

There were, however, a few bright spots in the history of the branch's attempt to implement its program. The branch's most productive activity came in the aftermath of the Chicago race riot of 1919. Initially, Brown and Bentley were uncertain as to whether even to get involved.[70] Their concern was for the branch's image and its respect for the law. Therefore, they sought to stay clear of any issue involving possible criminal

---

[65] *Chicago Defender,* 21 March 1914, p. 4.

[66] *Chicago Defender,* 13 March 1915, p. 1; and 22 May 1914, pp. 1, 12.

[67] *Chicago Defender,* 7 July 1917, p. 4.

[68] *Chicago Tribune,* 14 June 1916, p. 8.

[69] *Chicago Defender,* 27 January 1917, p. 12; 6 October 1917, p. 1; and 3 November 1917, p. 7.

[70] Waskow, *Race Riot,* 46, 47.

behavior on the part of blacks.[71] The branch's stance was not easy to understand since the actions of the local governments, both city and county, represented clear-cut cases of maladministration of justice.

After a visit to Chicago by Joel E. Spingarn, the national office directed the Chicago branch to enter the defense proceedings to protect the rights of the riot defendants, the bulk of whom were black. The national office saw in the riot and its aftermath a northern version of southern mob action. Something appeared amiss when 60 percent of all victims, including persons killed and injured, were black as well as more than 60 percent of the alleged perpetrators of violence. Once forced into action, the branch became the principal backer of the Joint Committee to Secure Equal Justice for Colored Riot Defendants. Branch secretary A.C. MacNeal, charged as a riot defendant after firing a gun into a mob outside his home, assumed the role of secretary to the ad hoc group. Support for the joint committee grew after former branch members Rosenwald, Addams, and Blaine lent their influence and gave sizeable financial contributions.

At the end of the first decade of its existence, the Chicago NAACP had not developed to its full potential. The ideology of egalitarianism, however, had taken root in fertile ground in black Chicago. In the decades to follow, the branch would grow while moving cautiously forward in pursuit of its goal of contributing locally to the creation of an egalitarian America.

---

[71] It is also possible that Brown and Bentley saw the defense of riot defendants as involving legal defense rather that legal redress, and the NAACP was mandated to attend to the latter only. See Kellogg, *NAACP,* 88.

Book Reviews

William Ashworth. *The Late, Great Lakes: An Environmental History.* New York: Knopf. 1986. Reprint. Detroit: Wayne State University Press. 1987. Pp. ix, 274. Paper $12.95.

Samuel de Champlain called them *mers douces,* "sweet seas." In their ocean-like vastness, they have always seemed infinite and undamageable. Yet the lakes are neither, and, in fact says William Ashworth, have now been brought to the brink of irreversible destruction.

In this provocative book, *The Late, Great Lakes: An Environmental History,* author Ashworth tells a compelling story of the lakes (or seas as he prefers to call them) from their geological formation to their present day environmental crisis.

The emphasis here is on the historical (as noted in the book's subtitle) and while no new environmental information is presented, the historical review is well done. Ashworth tells of what he calls resource extraction—the beaver, the great forests, the rich mines. Gone are the salmon, trout, and that "gift of the gods" the lake whitefish. They have been displaced by the sea lamprey, the alewife, and the smelt which entered the lakes through navigational canals dug in the nineteenth century.

We read of the "death" of Lake Erie which in a real sense, notes Ashworth, marked the rebirth of the modern environmental movement. The effects of rain, dumps, and superships are recounted as is the astonishing plan to pipe water from the lakes to the arid agricultural High Plains states.

Ashworth ends his account with a devastating attack on those of us who live in the Great Lakes states—it is our apathy that he fails to comprehend.

This is a well written book, with an excellent bibliography. Originally published in 1986, this reprint by Wayne State University Press, part of its fine Great Lakes Books series, unfortunately does not contain the endpaper maps of the original edition.

In all, William Ashworth has written a disturbing book. It is a book that should be read by anyone concerned with the history and the future of our Great Lakes.

Arthur M. Woodford
Director
St. Clair Shores Public Library
St. Clair Shores, Michigan

Andrew R. L. Cayton. *The Frontier Republic: Ideology and Politics in the Ohio Country, 1780-1825.* Kent State University Press. 1986. Pp. 209. $27.00.

The Frontier Republic is a local history only in terms of the geographical boundaries of the subject. Ohio was the first state (1803) carved from the federal domain created by the Revolutionary Settlement, and the first to pass through the stages of territorial tutelage prescribed by the Northwest Ordinance of 1787. Ohio's early years demonstrate the new nation's attempt to determine the part that the West would play in the future of the Republic. Cayton places his narrative squarely within the context of the ideological rift between Federalists and Republicans over the role of the federal government in state and local affairs and their competing visions of the West. Jeffersonian Republicans in early Ohio insisted upon "local sovereignty and personal autonomy" and saw the West as an "endless recreation of an agrarian world of independent farmers" (p. 12). Federalists advocated what Cayton neatly labels an "Empire of System" (in contrast to the Jeffersonian "Empire of Liberty") and called for an "urban, commercial West fully integrated into the Atlantic world and guided by a superintending national authority" (p. 21). The two visions proved long-lived. From the coalescence of the first party system to the formation of the second, issues of central versus local control, elite versus popular government, and economic regulation versus entrepreneurial initiative dominated Ohio politics. Both visions remained vital because neither triumphed. By the 1820s, Ohio had developed into both a society of independent, competing interests and an economy integrated into the international market.

The Frontier Republic is a gracefully written, valuable work that should be accessible to undergraduates. Nevertheless, with the exception of his chapter on Marietta which shows the literal formation of a Federalist landscape, Cayton is not completely successful in translating rhetoric into reality. Most discussion of social and economic change resides in one chapter on the boom-and-bust years following the War of 1812, yet Cayton's reading of the political rhetoric for the entire period emphasizes that frontier Ohioans were constantly either becoming pluralistic and individualistic or promoting government measures to mitigate such tendencies. In short, the behavioral evidence on which this work depends is too much assumed.

Susan E. Gray,
Middlebury College

Patricia Cooper. *Once a Cigar Maker: Men, Women, and Work Culture in American Cigar Factories, 1900-1919.* Urbana and Chicago: University of Illinois Press. 1987. Pp xvi, 350. $29.95.

Patricia Cooper's book, *Once a Cigar Maker,* merges the best of both old and new trends in American labor history. Cooper presents an incisive and detailed description of the work processes in the cigar making industry, the rise of the powerful Cigar Makers' International Union, and the relationship between this union and its predominantly male membership. But by bringing to her subject a new alertness to the presence of non-union women workers, who made the cheaper but very popular 'nickel' cigars, Cooper greatly expands our understanding of both the industry and its work force.

Combining local, state, and federal labor records with an intensive use of oral histories, Cooper compares the work cultures of male and female workers, and contrasts the central role of the union in male workers' lives with the more subtle influence of women's solidarities and traditions on the female cigar makers. In each case, Cooper argues, a militant tradition emerged, one that was powerfully molded by the work process itself.

Central to this book is Cooper's focus on the ways that gender divided the work force and prevented it from effectively fighting the changes that led to the union's demise. Looking at women workers in two case studies, on Polish workers in Detroit and on native-born workers in southeastern Pennsylvania, Cooper has increased our knowledge of the female sector of the workforce. By carefully analyzing the impact of gender as well as economic dynamics, she has also gained impressive new insights into male unionists, the workers labor historians have most often studied. Her discussion of how gender divisions affected unionists' craft exclusivism, for example, is extremely sophisticated. Thus *Once a Cigar Maker* is an excellent example of the pathbreaking influence women's history has begun to have on the way we perceive men, as well as women.

Julia Green
Yale University

Ronald Edsforth. *Class Conflict and Cultural Consensus: The Making of a Mass Consumer Society in Flint, Michigan.* New Brunswick and London: Rutgers University Press. 1987. Pp. 294. Cloth $40.00, paper $12.00.

If one purpose of history is to inform our understanding of the present and future, Ronald Edsforth's study of the ways in which automobile manufacturing transformed Flint during the first half of this century and of the cultural and political consensus that emerged there could not appear at a more appropriate time. Recent changes in the industry that still dominate Flint are reshaping the community and challenging the viability of that consensus. The book deserves a wide and careful reading because its analysis of the development of the complex series of compromises and "working agreements" that defined the nature of both community and political life in Flint during the rise of automobile manufacturing is very carefully drawn and may well be instructive to those faced with the same task during the contraction of that industry.

This is a somewhat difficult book to categorize because the focus is not on any one aspect of Flint—business, industry, labor, etc.—but on the interactions among the various segments of the community. This leads to a focus on local politics, the common ground on which the various segments of the community presented and advocated their particular needs.

The book is also difficult to deal with because of its almost militantly traditional methodology. Edsforth begins the book with a very direct statement of his methodology, "This study . . . is a very traditional history, not an exercise in historical social science" (p. ix). The return to narrative historical writing has been much heralded the last few years and many prominent historians have called for a greater attention to history as a form of literature. As in all attempts to redress an imbalance, the quantitative and social scientific models had perhaps become too dominant, there is the danger of overcorrection. Methodology need not, and should not, be an *a priori* conviction or a matter of faith. Methodology should flow from the particular questions the historian seeks to address and reflect the best way to analyze and use available sources. Edsforth's rejection of social scientific methodology rules out (at least as far as one can judge from what is in the text and notes) quantitative analysis of voting behavior or the characteristics of Flint's rapidly growing population. Given the attention devoted to local politics and the weight that the changing fortunes of particular politicians are asked to carry in the argument, such analysis would appear to have been highly appropriate. What it would have revealed and how it might have affected the thesis of the book is impossible to guess.

In the end, though, *Class Conflict and Cultural Consensus* must be addressed as it is rather than as it might have been. Edsforth presents a very careful and thorough analysis of the process by which Flint developed a workable common ground that allowed community and political life to flourish. The disruptions of rapid industrialization, growth in both population and demands for city services, and the physical expansion of the city all were subsumed in a series of "compacts" that have survived until the current restructuring of the industry and the corporation, that was the engine for change in Flint in the 20s and 30s and remains so today.

William H. Mulligan, Jr.
Clarke Historical Library
Central Michigan University

Conrad Hilberry. *Luke Karamazov.* Detroit, Michigan: Wayne State University Press. 1987. Pp. 189.

If Ralph Ray Searl were just another high school dropout, Conrad Hilberry admits that he would not have crossed town to speak to him, let alone have put up with considerable inconvenience to interview him, and others who knew him, over an extended period of time. What fascinates Hilberry about his subject is the same thing that will fascinate Hilberry's readers: Searl (or "Luke Karamazov," the highly literary name Searl adopts in prison) is ˌa multiple murderer and a psychopath.

Hilberry's study of Searl is difficult to categorize. It is not "new journalism" in the vein of Truman Capote's *In Cold Blood* because Hilberry makes no attempt to use the techniques of fiction to recreate Searl's story; it is not a psychoanalytical study, although Hilberry is obviously interested in the psychological aspects of his subject; it is not a criminalogical case history, although Ralph and his brother Tom are the major figures in one of the goriest chapters in the criminal history of Kalamazoo, Michigan; and it is not fiction, although it often reads as if it were a murder mystery.

Hilberry's profile of Ralph Ray Searl is a little of all of the above. It is also more. In this well-written account of a psychopathic personality, the author is probing our common humanity, especially its darker side, in ways reminiscent of many of the "dark" classics of modern literature. Searl is to Hilberry what Kurtz is to Marlow in Joseph Conrad's "Heart of Darkness."

In both cases a representative of the values most dear to the community confronts an individual whose values are destructive to that community. In both cases the errant individual has achieved a high social position in a different, more closed, social environment (prison, a cannibal tribe): and in both cases the implications and conclusions are similar. Much as we might like to see Searl as a moral monster, someone so unlike most of us that he seems almost a different breed, Hilberry insists on exploring those aspects of his character that connect him to us: intelligence, pride, integrity, even responsibility. Likewise, Conrad's Marlow insisted that Kurtz was not "mad."

Both Joseph Conrad and Conrad Hilberry seem preoccupied with "the fascination of the abomination" and both seem to be saying that the more we confront it the more we see of ourselves. Ralph Searl may have killed innocent victims for reasons that make no sense and he may have been incapable of coping with "normal" life; yet his actions, however irrational, were the result of the same kinds of desires to make our lives meaningful shared by all of us.

Hilberry's study of Ralph Ray Searl is ultimately a philosophical study. Relying heavily upon Ernest Becker's version of the major tenets of existential thought as they are outlined in *The Denial of Death,* Conrad Hilberry illustrates how even the criminal acts of a psychopath can be seen as understandable reactions to the human dilemma. Since we are blessed with remarkable powers of perception and imagination, each of us has a sense of "uniqueness and grandeur;" yet precisely because of these powers, we know that we are "dying animals." In order to live our lives at all, we have to be able to ignore our sense of our own mortality lest we be overcome by a sense of purposelessness and absurdity. The "drive of heroism, for cosmic recognition, even if it means suicide or murder" is one means by which we can temporarily repress our sense of our own mortality. The "reduction of the universe to a manageable size" is another. Fortunately for the life of communities, most of us manage the above without endangering the lives of others. Unfortunately for his victims in and around Kalamazoo, Ralph Searl did not. Conrad Hilberry's *Luke Karamazov* is a sympathetic study of the unfortunate ways that his psychopathic subject goes about finding his own form of heroism (murdering, lying, bullying) and reducing the universe to a size that allows him to control it (incarceration in prison). It is a fascinating portrayal; its fascination is at least partially due to Hilberry's refusal to stereotype or oversimplify his subject. As Emanuel Tanay suggests in his "Introduction," Ralph Searl's life seems far stranger and more outrageous than fiction.

Most of us know that the lines between fact and fiction, the rational and the irrational, the heroic and the foolish are thin indeed. Most of us also know that it has always been difficult truly to understand what it would be like to be someone else. When the someone else in question is a psychopathic multiple murderer, the difficulty is very great indeed. Conrad Hilberry is up to the task in a book that is both instructive and entertaining.

Stacy W. Thompson
Central Michigan University

Carol Kammen. *On Doing Local History: Reflections on What Local Historians Do, Why, and What It Means.* Nashville: The American Association for State and Local History. 1987. Pp. 184. Paper $13.50.

Unprecedented numbers of Americans are "doing" local history these days. Awakened to local and family history by recent celebrations beginning with the 1976 Independence Bicentennial, spurred on by innumerable state and local events, and led to family history by the "Roots" phenomenon and the Statue of Liberty restoration, amateur historians are researching, interviewing, writing, collecting, lecturing, video-taping, and doing exhibits as never before.

Based on its title, Carol Kammen's *On Doing Local History* would appear to be the ideal manual for these untrained, but highly motivated volunteers in Clio's legions. However, the title is misleading. This book concentrates on researching and writing local history, and its reflections are less what local historians do and more what Kammen thinks they should do. This limitation should be understood, and then *On Doing Local History* should be read by local historians, and kept close at hand as a reminder of what well researched and well written local history can contribute to a community and to the historical profession.

Kammen, a trained historian who has been doing local history in the Ithaca, New York, area for many years, begins with her definition of local history. It is, she says, "the study of past events, or of people or groups, in a given geographic area—a study based on a wide variety of documentary evidence and placed in a comparative context that should be both regional and national. This study, ought to be accomplished by a historian using methods appropriate to the topic under consideration."

This definition is essential to understanding Kammen's book and the reason it was written. She pointedly rejects narrow views of local history as the history of a community or a family, and reminds her readers that not only are there many highly trained historians who work outside an academic setting, but that there are many amateur historians who take a critical, analytical, imaginative, and professional approach to their work. These historians use the local perspective to study topics as diverse as workers' ethnicity, neighborhoods, and women. Kammen proposes twenty such topics that local historians might profitably consider; her goal is to acknowledge practitioners who share her definition of local history, while encouraging a broader vision on the part of those who "fail to identify questions that the discipline of history asks," and seek only to discover "what happened."

After an initial chapter titled "Local History and Local Historians" that reviews the practice of local history from the 1870s to the present, Kammen devotes the remainder of her book to suggestions for researching and writing local history. She argues for topical approaches rather than chronological narratives; suggests activities such as regional, cooperative projects; warns against occupational hazards like "booster" expectations and protecting privacy; and speaks positively about writing local history for the popular press.

On Doing Local History is a useful handbook for writing local history, and a good reminder for historians of the many resources and opportunities that the field presents. Local historians who heed Kammen's advice to explore new topics, strive for greater objectivity, seek popular audiences, and place their history in a larger context can expect recognition from their community and the personal work. As Kammen acknowledges when she discusses the snail's pace approachment with academic historians, recognition from their teaching peers will come more slowly.

Gordon L. Olson
Grand Rapids City Historian

John McCabe. *Grand Hotel Mackinac Island.* Sault Ste. Marie, Mich.: The Unicorn Press. 1987. Pp. xvii, 254. $29.95.

If this book contained merely a recitation of calamities that have befallen the Grand Hotel since it was built in 1887, it would still be interesting.

The Grand had a half-dozen changes in management in its first half-century as its owners struggled to make the hotel pay. With an operating season of less than three summer months, the hotel had plenty of time to lose money, little time to make it; year after year!

Owned by a troika of transportation companies, the Grand, still the world's largest summer hotel, was built in 100 days by Harbor Springs builder, C.W. Caskey, with the help of 300 carpenters, and, apparently, without the help of an architect.

The story of a succession of managers' struggles to keep it going is a highly readable one, sometimes funny, sometimes pathetic. At times the service personnel outnumbered the registered guests. The situation was aggravated, of course, when the huge building began to age and major overhaul expenses ran a race with normal operating costs. Once, during the Great Depression, the Grand was in receivership.

Fortunately, in 1919, W. Stewart Woodfill appeared on the scene in a small job, to begin his long association with the hotel. After several years through a remarkable series of events, he became sole owner. He improved the facility immensely, and put it on a paying basis. Woodfill died in 1984 after sixty-five years with the Grand Hotel.

Perhaps his most important legacy to his beloved hotel, island and state was the intensive, if sometimes onerous, training and guidance he gave to his nephew, Dan Musser, to follow in his footsteps. For several years Musser has been putting the Grand in apple-pie order for its centennial.

As measured by author McCabe, the hotel seems actually alive, and much younger than her one hundred years.

William H. Ohle
Horton Bay, MI.

Carol McGinnis. *Michigan Genealogy, Sources and Resources.* Baltimore: Genealogical Publishing Co. Inc. 1987. Pp. 110. $15.00.

Genealogy is no longer considered—indeed it never actually was—an eccentric pastime pursued by slightly daffy ancestor worshipers. Instead, genealogy is a legitimate avocation (in some cases even an academic discipline) requiring a high degree of energy, skill, and research ability. Michigan is fertile ground for family historians. Each year increasing numbers of genealogists visit the state's libraries, archives and court houses. The sesquicentennial year has encouraged even more individuals to seek out their family heritage. However, no reliable guide to genealogical research in Michigan has been available.

Carol McGinnis has solved the problem. This book is a carefully prepared manual which both the novice and experienced researcher will find very helpful. The author begins with a brief overview of Michigan history and a list of suggested readings. The real meat, however, is the extensive listings she provides of vital and county records, census schedules, land records, genealogical collections and historical and genealogical societies. The bulk of this information is provided by county, making it an easy-to-use practical research tool.

The book must, however, be used with some caution. Most of the included data, gathered by letters to county offices, libraries, and societies, was not verified in-person by the author. Therefore, some may be out-of-date or erroneous. A genealogist should always call or write before making a research trip to be sure that the records sought are actually available.

With this book the author and publisher have met a conspicuous research need, for which the state's genealogists will for many years be thankful.

Richard J. Hathaway
Senior Consultant
Public Policy Research
Public Sector Consultants
Lansing

Edward Nicholas. *The Chaplain's Lady: Life and Love at Fort Mackinac.* Mackinac Island, Mich.: Mackinac Island State Park Commission. 1987. Illustrated. Pp. vi, 82. $5.00.

Nineteen-year-old Charlotte Tull came to America from her native England in 1832 following a decline in the family fortunes at home. Late that year she and her brothers reached Monroe, Michigan, where she later met the Reverend John O'Brien. A native Irishman, O'Brien had emigrated several years previously and received ordination as an Episcopalian minister. The couple married in 1836 and six years later O'Brien was appointed chaplain to the garrison at Fort Mackinac. He retained that position until the troops were withdrawn from the island in 1861. He later ministered to a parish at Pontiac until his death in 1864, nearly ten years after that of his wife.

In this slender volume—really an extended article—Edward Nicholas explores the history of this couple, his great-grandparents, and their three children. He bases his work largely on family correspondence. Quotations account for nearly a third of his text. About three-fourths of the material relates to the period at Mackinac. In the process of recounting everyday events and family crises he explores the tensions that arose from this marriage between the rather emotional Charlotte and her austere and intellectual husband. At the same time he examines middle-class marriage roles during the mid-nineteenth century, noting Charlotte's ultimate conformity to the convention of female passivity in compliance with the directives of the dominant male.

The professional historian will find little of interest here. For the general reader, however, it offers interesting insights into family life in nineteenth-century Mackinac through the medium of clearly etched individual personalities. The profusion of illustrations of both the O'Brien family and of Mackinac itself will further enhance its popular appeal as will the author's fluent pen and occasional romantic embellishment of his subjects.

Richard G. Bremer
Hoboken, NJ

Steven J. Ross. *Workers on the Edge. Work, Leisure, and Politics in Industrializing Cincinnati, 1788-1890.* (Columbia History of Urban Life Series.) New York: Columbia University Press. 1985. Pp. xx, 406. $37.50.

Steven Ross begins his excellent study in working class history by reminding us that there were more strikes and more people killed or wounded in labor demonstrations in the United States in the two decades after 1876 than in any other country in the world. He then proceeds to explain why, in spite of this unrest, workers were unable to develop a class consciousness and unity that was able to foster appropriate political, social, and economic change. Although he cites a variety of reasons, the author focuses on the social, ethnocultural, and political differences among the workers themselves as the chief culprits.

The book is divided into three parts; the Age of the Artisan (1788-1843); the Age of Manufacturing (1843-1873); and the Age of Modern Industry (1873-1890). Each part explores the varied and complex process of economic change, and traces the reactions of workers to this change, not just as workers, but as citizens who "took seriously the republican heritage of the American Revolution. . . ." (p. xix). By the 1880s, he notes, workers perceived industrial capitalism as not only subverting the rights of workers, but as threatening the ideals of the Republic. As a result, workers put aside their differences and united as citizens in a series of both labor and political movements which, if they had succeeded, would have changed the course of industrialization. However "unresolvable cleavages. . . within the labor movement over the relationship between the individual worker and the industrial system," doomed the brief period of unity (p. 316).

This thoughtful and well-written book is a joy to read. It successfully combines the new labor history with an effective narrative, and convincingly tells a story whose importance goes far beyond the boundaries of Cincinnati. Indeed, scholars of Michigan's urban, social, and labor history would do well to consult this work.

Robert B. Fairbanks
University of Texas
at Arlington

Book Notes

Wayne State University Press is publishing a series of reprints of books dealing with Michigan history. These "Great Lakes Books" include the following.

Romig, Walter. *Michigan Place Names: The History of the Founding and the Naming of More Than Five Thousand Past and Present Michigan Communities.* 1973. Reprint. Detroit, Mich.: Wayne State University Press. 1986. Pp. 673. Cloth, $45.00, paper, $15.00.

This book covers Michigan towns and cities from Aabec to Zutphen. A brief history of more than 5,000 place names is provided. Romig spent more than a decade collecting the information for his book. The short sketches of the origins of Michigan's geographical names are supplemented with an extensive index of the personal names mentioned in the accounts. The book should be in every public library in the state. It will also be of interest to Michigan travelers, genealogists, and historians.

Catton, Bruce. *Waiting for the Morning Train: An American Boyhood.* 1972. Reprint. Detroit, Mich.: Wayne State University Press. 1987. Pp. xvi, 260. Cloth, $24.50, paper, $9.95.

This is a nostalgic account of growing up in Benzonia in Benzie County in the early years of this century. Catton, the great historian of the Civil War, recalls the time of his youth in a northern Michigan town. Catton's superb writing style and his lively stories of life in Benzonia make this book pleasant reading for anyone interested in Michigan history.

Lewis, David L. *The Public Image of Henry Ford: An American Folk Hero and His Company.* 1976. Reprint. Detroit, Mich.: Wayne State University Press, 1987. Pp. 599. Paper $14.95.

Professor David Lewis probably knows more about Henry Ford and the Ford Motor Company than any other writer. In this volume Lewis covers the impact made by Ford and his company on the American public. He studies the advertising and public relations of Ford throughout the pioneer automaker's career. The book is well-written and well-researched.

****

Other recent publications include:

Barnett, LeRoy. *Railroads in Michigan: A Catalogue of Company Publications, 1836-1980.* Marquette, Mich.: Northern Michigan University Press. 1986. Pp. xviii, 180. Paper $13.50.

LeRoy Barnett, Reference Archivist for the Bureau of Michigan History, has compiled a checklist of publications issued by Michigan railroads from 1836 to 1980. The location of these publications in public libraries is also noted. The checklist includes annual reports, tourist literature and other types of publicity, labor contracts, rulebooks, and mortgages. The work will be of value to railroad buffs, archivists, and librarians.

Perry, W. Hawkins. *The Legacy of Albert Kahn.* With an essay by William B. Sanders. 1970. Reprint. Detroit, Mich.: Wayne State University Press. 1987. Illustrated. Pp. 183. Paper $14.95.

This book was originally published as a catalogue to accompany an exhibition of the works of the noted architect, Albert Kahn, at the Detroit Institute of Arts in 1970. Along with brief sketches of the works of Kahn and the Kahn Associates, the book contains more than 200 photographs of Kahn's buildings and drawings.

Great Pages of Michigan History from the Detroit Free Press. Bill McGraw, compiler. Detroit, Mich.: *Detroit Free Press* and Wayne State University Press. 1987. Illustrated. Pp. 196. Paper $14.95.

Represented here are reproductions of the top stories in the *Detroit Free Press* for more than 150 years. One can find accounts of the death of Father Gabriel Richard, the founding of the Republican party at Jackson, the election of Frank Murphy as governor in 1930, the assassination of John Kennedy, the opening of the Renaissance Center, and much more.

McCollum, Anita. *Come Explore Michigan the Beautiful.* Au Train, Mich.: Avery Color Studios. 1986. Illustrated. Pp. 80. Paper $8.95.

Intended as a text for children in the middle primary grades, this book has brief essays on some of the major historic and geographical sites in Michigan. The text is supplemented with a great number of full-color photographs.

Massie, Larry, ed. *From Frontier Folk to Factory Smoke: Michigan's First Century of Historical Fiction.* Au Train, Mich.: Avery Color Studios. 1987. Pp. 280. Paper $7.49.

Larry Massie has studied a large number of novels dealing with Michigan life and has selected excerpts from sixteen books written between 1839 and 1925 for this anthology. A brief introduction precedes each selection.

Williams, Meade. *Early Mackinac: A Sketch Historical and Descriptive.* 1897. Reprint. Au Train, Mich.: Avery Color Studios. 1987: Pp. 184. Paper $7.49.

The Rev. Meade C. Williams first published his collection of the history and the stories of Mackinac Island in 1897. Revised and expanded versions of the book were published in 1901, 1903, and 1912. Of particular value in this new edition of the book is Larry Massie's seventeen-page bibliographical essay on "The Literature of Mackinac County."

****

As a matter of policy, the *Michigan Historical Review* will not review books published by the Clarke Historical Library. This is to avoid even the appearance of a conflict of interest. We do, however, want to make our readers aware of such titles. We will list such titles in our book notes section with a brief description.

Meints, Graydon M. *Along the Tracks: A Directory of Named Places on Michigan Railroads.* Mount Pleasant, Mich.: Clarke Historical Library. 1987. Cloth $25.00, paper $15.00.

A listing of all named places along the various railroad lines in Michigan that is arranged by county and provides, where known, township coordinates and mileage points on the rail line or lines serving the community, Meints' book will be useful to genealogists and local historians as well as railroad researchers.

Editor's Page

A small number of copies of Vol. 13, No. 2 were incorrectly bound at the printer. In some copies pages 60 to 65 are either missing or duplicated. If you have a damaged copy, please return it to the editor for a free exchange.

****

Call for Papers. The Tenth Annual North American Labor History Conference, scheduled 20-22 October 1988, at Wayne State University is seeking proposals for papers, sessions, special events, and featured speakers. The program committee envisions sessions reflective of the best of recent scholarship in the diverse areas of labor history. It is hoped that the program will include sessions dealing with Canadian and European labor history, as well as American. Proposals relating to other geographical areas are also welcome. The deadline is 1 June 1988. Please contact:

> Christopher H. Johnson
> Department of History
> Wayne State Unviersity
> Detroit, Michigan 48202

****

In Vol. 13, No. 2 the author of *Golden Wheels* was incorrectly spelled in the Book Review section. The correct spelling is Richard Wager.

Great Lakes Books, an Imprint of
Original and Classic Regional Titles from

WAYNE STATE UNIVERSITY PRESS

Now Available in Paperback

An Afternoon in Waterloo Park

By Gerald Dumas.
"This uniquely American memoir hits a universal nerve."—Helen DelMonte, *McCall's.* Impelled by his mother's death, Dumas contemplates three generations of his family and lyrically records his impressions of life on Dickerson Avenue in Detroit. *Waterloo Park* is a complex story, recollected from the surface of childhood and pondered from the depths of mature experience.
140 pages, illustrated, 5¼ x 8   April
ISBN 0-8143-2038-4   cloth, $19.95
ISBN 0-8143-2039-2   paper, $9.95

Hemingway in Michigan

By Constance Cappel.
"The author has identified places and people with surprising precision . . . worth reading."—The Saturday Review. Cappel chronicles Hemingway's adventures at his family's summer cottage on Walloon Lake in northern Michigan. In uncovering the pattern of compulsive returns Hemingway made to the area, the book provides insight to understanding Hemingway's life and his writing.
244 pages, illustrated   March
ISBN 0-8143-2059-7 cloth, $25.00
ISBN 0-8143-2060-0 paper. $12.95

Detroit Perspectives

Crossroads and Turning Points

Edited by Wilma Henrickson.
Henrickson's collection of documents focuses on significant turning points in the history of Detroit. Spanning the time from before statehood to the present, the decisive moments form a unique chronology on the shaping of the city.
300 pages   September
ISBN 0-8143-2013-9   cloth, $29.95
ISBN 0-8143-2014-7   paper, $12.95

Miracle Bridge at Mackinac

By David B. Steinman. In Collaboration with John T. Nevill. Foreword by G. Mennen Williams. Drawings and Etchings by Reynold H. Weidnaar. Here is a first-hand account of the world's longest suspension bridge, told by the engineer who masterfully designed the bridge and by the reporter who watched it become a reality.
226 pages, illustrated   August
ISBN 0-8143-2042-2   cloth, $22.50
ISBN 0-8143-2043-0   paper, $10.95

Order from your bookstore or directly from

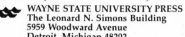

WAYNE STATE UNIVERSITY PRESS
The Leonard N. Simons Building
5959 Woodward Avenue
Detroit, Michigan 48202
(313) 577-6120